A Vulnerable America

An Overview of National Security

A Vulnerable America

An Overview of National Security

THE
LUCENT
LIBRARY OF
HOMELAND
SECURITY

A Vulnerable America
An Overview of National Security

Geoffrey A. Campbell

LUCENT
BOOKS®

THOMSON
GALE

San Diego • Detroit • New York • San Francisco • Cleveland • New Haven, Conn. • Waterville, Maine • London • Munich

To MacKenzie, Kirby, and the students of Dunbar Middle School.

© 2004 by Lucent Books. Lucent Books is an imprint of The Gale Group, Inc.,
a division of Thomson Learning, Inc.

Lucent Books® and Thomson Learning™ are trademarks used herein under license.

For more information, contact
Lucent Books
27500 Drake Rd.
Farmington Hills, MI 48331-3535
Or you can visit our Internet site at http://www.gale.com

LIBRARY OF CONGRESS CATALOGING-IN-PUBLICATION DATA

Campbell, Geoffrey A.
    A vulnerable America / by Geoffrey A. Campbell.
        v. cm. — (the Lucent library of homeland security)
Includes bibliographical references and index.
Contents: Safeguarding the nation's transportation system—Bracing for bioterrorism and
other weapons—Racial profiling and the battle against terrorism—A consolidation of
power—A changing way of life.
    ISBN 1-59018-383-5 (hardback: alk. paper)
1. Civil defense—United States—Juvenile literature. 2. Terrorism—United States—
Prevention—Juvenile literature. 3. National security—United States—Juvenile literature.
4. United States—Defenses—Juvenile literature. [1. Civil defense. 2. Terrorism—Prevention.
3. National security.] I. Title. II. Series.
UA927.C35 2004
363.3'2'0973—dc21

                                                                2003008150

Printed in the United States of America

Contents

Foreword

Stunned by the terrorist attacks of September 11, 2001, millions of Americans clung to President George W. Bush's advice in a September 20 live broadcast speech to "live your lives, and hug your children." His soothing words made an indelible impression on people in need of comfort and paralyzed by fear. Recent history had seen no greater emotional flood than occurred in the days following September 11, as people were united by deep shock and grief and an instinctive need to feel safe.

Searching for safety, a panicked nation urged taking extreme and even absurd measures. Immediately after the attacks, it was suggested that all aircraft passengers be restrained for the duration of flights—better to restrict the movement of all than to risk allowing one dangerous passenger to act. After the attempted bombing of a flight from Paris to Atlanta in December 2001, one *New York Times* columnist even half-seriously suggested starting an airline called Naked Air—"where the only thing you wear is a seat belt." Although such acute fear and paranoia waned as the attacks slipped further into the past, a dulled but enduring desire to overhaul national security remained.

Creating the Department of Homeland Security was one way to allay citizens' panic and fear. Congress has allocated billions to secure the nation's infrastructure, bolster communication channels, and protect precious monuments against terrorist attack. Further funding has equipped emergency responders with state-of-the-art tools such as hazardous-material suits and networked communication systems. Improved databases and intelligence-gathering tools have extended the reach of intelligence agencies, in the effort to ferret out the terrorists hiding among us. Supporters of these programs praised the Bush administration for its attention to security lapses and agreed that in the post–September 11 world, only with tighter security could Americans go about their lives free of fear and reservation.

It did not take long, however, for the sense of national unity and purpose to splinter as people advanced countless ideas for actually achieving that security. As it became evident that ensuring safety meant curtailing Americans' freedom, the price of security became a hotly debated issue. With September 11 now years in the past, and after new wars and aggression waged in its name, it is not clear that the United States is any closer to becoming what many consider impossible: an America immune to attack. As distinguished political science professor Janice Gross Stein maintains, "Military preeminence, no matter how overwhelming, does not buy the United States security from attack, even in its heartland." Whether the invasion of sovereign nations, the deaths of thousands of civilians, and the continued endangerment of American troops have made the world any safer or the United States any less vulnerable to terror is unproved.

All Americans want to feel safe; beyond that basic agreement, however, commonality ends. Thus, how to ensure homeland security, and a myriad of related questions, is one of the most compelling and controversial issues in recent history. The books in this series explore this new chapter in history and examine its successes and challenges. Annotated bibliographies provide readers with ideas for further research, while fully documented primary and secondary source quotations enhance the text. Each book in the series carefully considers a different aspect of homeland security; together they provide students with a wealth of information as well as launching points for further study and discussion.

America Under Fire: A History of Response

Although the United States was viewed as the world's lone superpower at the beginning of the twenty-first century, the September 11, 2001, terrorist attacks demonstrated that the United States continued to face threats to its stability and prosperity. Such dangers have been with the nation since its founding in 1776. Though the source of the threats has changed over the years, one constant has been the tension between preserving the unique civil liberties enjoyed by American citizens and the need to protect those citizens from outside threats. Sometimes civil liberties are suspended in the name of national protection.

Several prime examples of that tension are evident in the policies of President Abraham Lincoln, who is regarded today as one of the finest chief executives the nation has ever known. Among other things, during the Civil War, Lincoln unilaterally suspended the writ of habeas corpus, a major constitutional protection against false imprisonment and illegal detention without a judicial hearing. Lincoln also made it a military offense for anyone, including civilians, to obstruct military enlistment or offer any sort of aid to the Confederate cause. Lincoln's rationale on both accounts was that the nation's very existence had been threatened by the secession movement of Southern states, and extreme measures were necessary to preserve the union.

Likewise, during World War I, Congress enacted laws that made it illegal to interfere with military recruitment or to make statements critical of the nation's war effort. The government convicted many people for disloyal speech and sedition, defending its actions by taking the position that extraordinary measures were necessary in order to ensure the nation's security.

Perhaps one of the most notorious examples of the lengths to which the U.S. government has gone to protect the nation from a perceived threat came during World War II. After the Japanese military bombed the U.S. naval installation at Pearl Harbor in Hawaii, the nation was anxious. Fearing further attacks, the government rounded up some 120,000 Japanese Americans and placed them in internment camps. All people of Japanese ancestry were placed in the camps, even those born in the United States. None were

After the Japanese bombing of Pearl Harbor during World War II, racism against Japanese Americans was rampant in the United States.

A Japanese American girl and her parents are transported to a detention center. All Japanese Americans, regardless of age, were considered a threat to national security.

afforded a trial to determine whether they were indeed national security threats. The government had decided that national security interests outweighed civil liberties.

Civil liberties were likewise compromised for the sake of national security during the Cold War between the United States and the Soviet Union. Americans who expressed liberal political views often were branded Communists and consequently were denied employment. A pervasive fear that the Soviet Union was attempting to sabotage the government by honeycombing it with agents led the government to force employees to take loyalty oaths, and ultimately led some government officials and lawmakers on campaigns to find and expose alleged Communists in government and other walks of life.

While such measures made many Americans uneasy, the governmental policies were supported by others who reasoned that the nation's citizens would lose all their rights if hostile foreign powers were successful in taking over the government. As Supreme Court chief justice William H. Rehnquist noted, "Without question the government's authority to engage in conduct that infringes civil liberty is greatest in time of declared war."[1]

In the immediate aftermath of the 2001 terrorist attacks, the government faced an enemy unlike any the United States had ever faced before. This new challenge has prompted the implementation of a variety of new weapons that range from enhanced law enforcement and information-gathering tools to restrictions on the movements of American citizens. Although designed ostensibly to ward off future terrorist attacks and tailored to avoid some of the infringements on civil liberties that characterized government efforts in earlier wars, critics worry that the new governmental powers hold the potential to significantly erode the personal freedoms and privacy of American citizens. Complicating the issue is the fact that no one knows how long the nation's war on terrorism will last. Consequently, critics warn, the erosion of basic civil liberties could continue for years. It remains to be seen how much of a reduction of liberty the American people and the courts will allow, but one thing is clear: The government faces a difficult task in trying to balance America's cherished civil liberties while simultaneously decreasing the nation's vulnerability to future terrorist attacks.

Chapter One

Safeguarding the Nation's Transportation System

The transportation system in the United States has been one of the nation's greatest resources, a vast network of airports, roadways, rail lines, and waterways that move millions of people daily and billions of dollars worth of goods each year. This free flow of people and commerce has become a hallmark of American life, helping to fuel the world's largest economy. The terrorist attacks of September 11, 2001, however, dramatically demonstrated the vulnerability of the nation's transportation system to terrorist infiltration and attack. They also demonstrated the impact such a crisis could have on the economy and the enormous difficulties involved in trying to safeguard such a far-flung and highly accessible system.

Following the September 11 tragedy, the government took quick steps to examine the safety of the nation's transportation system and to improve security in the air, on the nation's highways, bridges, tunnels and rails, and in the country's waterways and ports. Some of the government's responses were largely symbolic, intended to restore the public's confidence. Other governmental actions targeted specific safety shortcomings. All of the new safeguards were intended to make sure terrorists could never again use the nation's transportation system as a weapon.

Changes at the Nation's Airports

Because commercial airliners were used in the 2001 attacks, the airline industry felt the biggest and most immediate impact of the government's efforts. Creating a greater law enforcement presence at the nation's airports was among the first things done. President George W. Bush asked the nation's governors to install the National Guard at airports. Many Americans for the first time saw armed soldiers patrolling civilian areas. For many, the guardsmen's presence offered reassurance in the wake of the terrorist attacks, a feeling that no one would dare hazard an attack in the midst of so much obvious security. Others, however, felt a sense of unease. For these Americans, the idea of armed soldiers at airports conjured up images of military states, not the open and free United States. The federal government paid for the deployment, which included training in airport security techniques from the Federal Aviation Administration.

The deployment of guardsmen was a temporary measure implemented while the government considered more permanent methods to bolster airport security. Just two months after the terrorist attacks, Congress approved sweeping legislation, the Aviation and Transportation Security Act, which created a new federal agency called the Transportation Security Administration (TSA). The agency was charged with federalizing security, that is, making security the responsibility of the federal government, at the nation's 429 commercial airports. The TSA took over security operations that previously had been run by private commercial companies. It hired forty-four thousand screeners for the airports and, in an effort to attract a more qualified pool of applicants, the government offered higher pay and health benefits. The screeners also were required to undergo thorough background checks and to speak fluently in English.

In ways both subtle and striking, the heightened security made air travel vastly different for Americans than it had been prior to September 11, 2001. Today, the heightened security takes effect even before a passenger steps into the secure area of the airport.

Baggage Thoroughly Screened

All checked baggage—suitcases and other items passengers do not personally carry on to the planes—is now given a thorough screening. Screeners use a number of methods to ascertain the bags are free of explosives. Among the most common is an Explosives Detection System (EDS), a large device similar to a doctor's CAT-scan machine. Baggage is loaded onto the machine's conveyor belt, which may be

Al-Qaeda terrorists used hijacked airplanes as weapons of destruction in the 2001 attacks on the World Trade Center (pictured) and Pentagon.

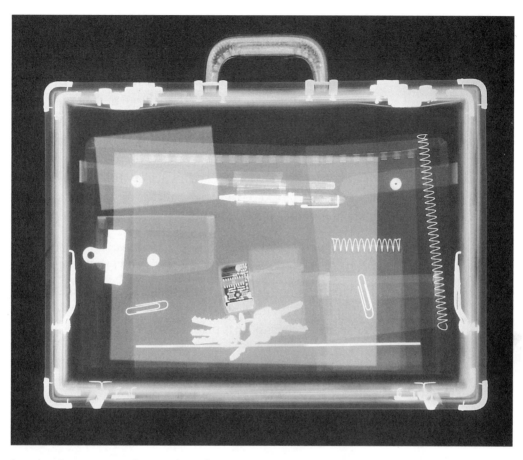

longer than twenty feet and, as the conveyor belt moves, the machine tests the molecular composition of the luggage's contents. The systems are based on the principle that explosives contain certain chemical elements in characteristic ratios and amounts that set them apart from nondangerous substances. Items placed in the machines are bombarded with neutrons. The resulting chemical reactions are analyzed by the machines to determine whether explosives are present.

An X-ray of a briefcase reveals its contents. Airport personnel can identify concealed weapons from such X-rays.

Another common machine in use at airports is the Explosives Trace Detection (ETD) machine, a much smaller device. Screeners rub the surface or interior of a traveler's luggage with chemically treated swabs, which are then placed into the ETD. The machine analyzes the samples for traces of bomb residue, utilizing similar principles to the EDS. The two machines are often used in tandem; if a bag that has run through the EDS raises concerns, it is then sent for ETD testing. Screeners also make use of bomb-sniffing dogs, though the dogs tire quickly when checking large numbers of bags. Airlines also utilize hand searches at times; the government has requested that passengers keep their luggage unlocked. According to traveling tips from the TSA, "You may keep your bag locked if you choose, but TSA is not liable for damage caused to locked bags that must be opened for security purposes."[2]

More Intense Passenger Screening

Heightened security measures do not stop at baggage screening. Travelers themselves are subject to screening at passenger security checkpoints prior to entering the gate areas of

A baggage screener inspects the contents of a man's luggage as part of the airport security process. All baggage must undergo a thorough screening process.

airports. Unlike in the past, when family and friends could accompany fliers to their gates, gate access is severely restricted. Only civilians with boarding passes and photo identification, and airport and airline employees who have valid identification cards, are allowed into the gate areas of airports. In addition, passengers and their carry-on luggage are subject to more thorough screening procedures than had been utilized in the past. Even food that passengers are munching on as they enter the secure areas must be screened: It is wrapped and run through an X-ray machine.

The first step of the security checkpoints is the X-ray machine, on which passengers are required to place all carry-on luggage, coats, jackets, and sealed food items. The procedure is intended to prevent passengers from boarding planes with any items that could be used as weapons. Because the only weapons used in the September 11 hijackings were box cutters, the government has significantly expanded the list of items that are not allowed in carry-on baggage. Prohibited items range from the fairly obvious, such as guns, knives, and explosives, to seemingly innocuous items that conceivably could be used as weapons, such as metallic pointed-tip scissors, box cutters, and sporting goods ranging from baseball bats and pool cues to ski poles. Passengers then walk through a metal detector. If an alarm is triggered, a passenger is subject to additional screening, during which a hand wand—another metal detector—is swept over the passenger's body.

Screeners may also pat down certain passengers, or request that they remove their shoes, which will be checked for explosives and either X-rayed or inspected with an ETD. The government became concerned about bombs concealed in footwear on December 21, 2001, after Richard Reid, a British national who allied himself with radical Muslim terrorist groups, attempted to blow up a commercial airliner en route to the United States. Reid, who became known as the "shoe bomber," carried on board a homemade explosive concealed in his shoes. He was subdued by passengers when he tried to ignite the material and sentenced to life in prison for

Metal detectors, both the walk-through system and handheld wands, are a crucial part of the passenger screening process.

attempted murder, attempted use of a weapon of mass destruction, attempted homicide, interfering with a flight crew, planting an explosive device on an airplane, attempted destruction of an aircraft, and using a destructive device in a crime of violence. Although Reid's conviction was a triumph, officials realized that further efforts had to be made to improve passenger prescreening systems.

CAPPS Analyzes Passengers

Security officials have systematic ways to pick out selected passengers for secondary screening procedures. They do this using a program known as Computer Assisted Passenger Prescreening System, or CAPPS. CAPPS helps security officials isolate passengers who may pose a security threat by culling information from both public and secret government sources and comparing it against governmental profiles of terrorists. For example, the system identifies people who purchase airline tickets with cash, buy one-way tickets, or have names similar to those of known terrorists, alerting security personnel to subject such people to heightened scrutiny. CAPPS had been in operation on September 11, 2001, and actually identified six of the September 11 hijackers as potential threats. However, they were subject only to a more thorough screening of their luggage, which contained no weapons. Those now identified by CAPPS are subject to a more thorough secondary screening.

Although CAPPS has the potential to identify terrorists, it often creates problems for law-abiding passengers. A Rochester, New York, man named Asif Iqbal, for example,

Computer scanning tickets helps airline personnel select passengers for secondary screening procedures.

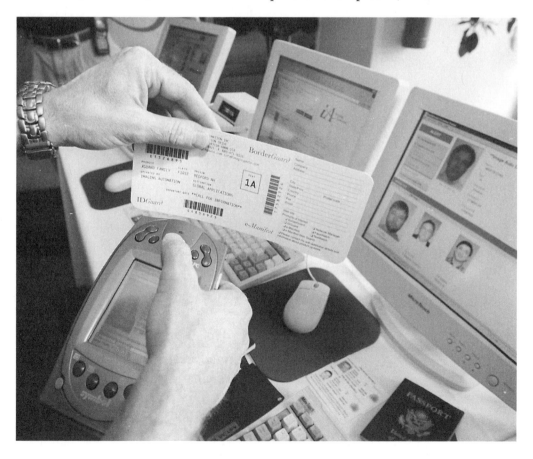

was required to get clearance from the Federal Bureau of Investigation (FBI) every time he flew, which he did sometimes as often as twice a week. Iqbal, a management consultant, had been singled out for scrutiny because he had the same name as a suspected terrorist. Even though that terrorism suspect was eight years younger than the Rochester man, and had been in U.S. custody at the naval base in Guantánamo Bay, Cuba, since 2002, Iqbal was detained at airports until finally receiving clearance from the FBI. Iqbal was hardly alone in his difficulties with CAPPS. Hundreds of Americans, ranging from a sixty-two-year-old grandmother to a frequent business traveler with a top-secret government security clearance, complained about being subjected to unnecessarily intense screening.

Despite such complaints, on February 28, 2003, the TSA announced that it had built an upgraded passenger pre-screening system called CAPPS II. This system relies on information gathered when passengers book a flight. A passenger's full name, address, phone number, and date of birth are used to access a vast amount of personal information—including credit and financial information, criminal records, and even property tax records—and are compared against current intelligence information and threat priorities. The information is then entered into a database and used to develop a risk assessment for each passenger. According to some reports, the government plans to develop a color-coded system to indicate the level of scrutiny each passenger should receive. For example, a passenger who is coded green would be subject to normal security screening, and those coded yellow would be subject to greater scrutiny. Those coded red are considered highly likely to pose a threat to security and would effectively be barred from flying.

Privacy and civil rights advocates complain that the current CAPPS system is problematic enough and that the new system is likely to be worse. David Sobel, a lawyer with the Electronic Privacy Information Center, worries about the quality of information fed into the database: "Looking ahead to the CAPPS II system, that system will likely have access to a broad pool of information that is unlikely to be completely accurate. We will see an exponential increase in the number of people who will encounter . . . problems."[3] A person who is mistakenly labeled red will face huge obstacles in trying to clear his or her identity. Other critics worry about the implications of allowing the government to concentrate large amounts of personal information, fearing such power might be used irresponsibly.

The new and enhanced security measures already have extended the boarding process to as long as two hours. Nevertheless, most Americans have been patient and have welcomed the added security. How patient and understanding they will remain is uncertain, especially considering the TSA's proposals to beef up security throughout airports, not just at entries to airline gates.

To offset lengthy backlogs at the checkpoints, the government is examining proposals that would allow prescreened frequent travelers to enjoy expedited security screening at airports. However, some worry that such a program could actually decrease security in the long term. A General Accounting Office study noted, for example, that the TSA initially opposed the concept because "of the potential for members of 'sleeper cells'—terrorists who spend time in the United States building up a law-abiding record—to become registered travelers in order to take advantage of less stringent security screening."[4] Such potential problems underscore the difficulties faced by the government as it attempts to balance security needs with the public's desire for ease of access at the nation's airports.

Safety in the Air

In addition to the vast increase in airport security, the government has instituted a variety of changes to increase safety once planes are aloft. Among the first priorities was to strengthen cockpit doors to prevent hijackers from gaining access. Prior to the September 11 attacks, most cockpit doors were relatively flimsy and could not be locked. They were designed solely to provide pilots with a quiet working environment. After the attacks, existing doors were reenforced with metal bars while improved doors were designed and produced. By early 2003, all large commercial planes flying in the United States were outfitted with lockable, bulletproof cockpit doors. The new doors are even capable of withstanding small explosions. A spokesman for the Boeing Company, maker of the new doors, claimed the improved doors were made to resist a force equal to that of a National Football League linebacker, running at the speed of an Olympic-class sprinter, before slamming into it.

Although the new doors have been hailed by supporters as a significant safety improvement, critics warn that the

A knife-wielding sky marshal simulates an airplane hijacking. Sky marshals are authorized to use lethal force against hijackers.

doors remain vulnerable. For example, if a pilot leaves the cockpit to make a visual inspection of the plane, the cockpit remains susceptible to attack. Captain Steve Luckey, the chairman of the Air Line Pilots Association's national security committee, observed of the improved door that "it's a barrier when it's closed, it's an entry when it's open."[5] Luckey and others have urged authorities to outfit airplanes with an additional bulletproof curtain to act as another barrier between the cockpits and cabins of planes. Others have argued for the installation of a second bulletproof door. Pilots would have to close one door before opening the other, reducing the vulnerability of the cockpit to attack.

The government has also increased the number of plainclothes federal air marshals on duty. Called sky marshals, these armed guards ride on selected flights and are authorized to use deadly force against hijackers. The enormous number of flights prevents the government from placing a sky marshal on every flight, but the odds have significantly increased that an armed law enforcement official is on any given flight. For security purposes, the government does not reveal the exact number of sky marshals, their identities, or the routes the marshals fly.

Many pilots believed that even these extraordinary efforts were insufficient in the face of a determined hijacking attempt, and they lobbied Congress for authorization to carry guns in the cockpit. Opponents of the idea argued that, in the event of a hijacking, pilots should focus on maintaining control of the aircraft. They also expressed concern over the possibility that pilots might inadvertently damage or incapacitate a plane through faulty shooting. Lawmakers, however, were finally won over by the pilots' argument that thousands of air travelers daily showed implicit trust in pilots simply by getting on planes. As debate raged in Congress, the Allied Pilots Association posted a petition on its website that said, "Common sense and logic dictate that the men and women we trust each day with our lives when we board an airliner can and should be trusted with firearms in order to provide the critical last line of defense."[6]

Sensitive to the controversy, some airlines sought to arm their pilots with nonlethal Taser stun guns. In January 2003, United Airlines and Mesa Airlines applied for approval from the TSA to allow their pilots to carry the weapons, which would incapacitate, but not kill, would-be hijackers and terrorists, and would be less likely to cause structural damage to the aircraft.

The presence of guns in the cockpit represents a change in the method pilots will now use during hijacking attempts. Prior to September 11, the standard procedure for pilots was to submit to hijackers' demands. The rationale was that, by acceding to the hijackers' requests, the lives of innocent passengers could be spared. Since the airliners themselves were used as missiles in the 2001 attacks, however, the government and pilots recognized that a much more aggressive approach was necessary in order to preserve control of the aircraft and improve the odds of survival. Indeed, in the wake of the attacks, the Defense Department authorized fighter pilots to shoot down hijacked planes, in effect sacrificing the lives of those on board to save the thousands who might be killed if the planes are flown into buildings.

Security for Ground Transportation

Though the nation's air transportation system was the most obvious area in need of improvement following the September 11 attacks, government officials and private analysts also began to examine the country's ground transportation system. As officials hypothesized potential terrorist scenarios involving ground transportation, they came to chilling conclusions. Among other things, they realized that terrorists could gain control of a hazardous shipment and drive it into a public building or otherwise use it to cause panic and commotion. Government officials also worried that terrorists could learn to drive large trucks, load them with explosives, and similarly wreak havoc.

Recognizing the danger of terrorists who might infiltrate their industry, the American Trucking Association in 2002

A California Highway Patrol officer thoroughly inspects a truck as part of the tighter security regulations for ground transportation.

lobbied for the right to conduct federal government background tests on drivers, dock workers, and job applicants. Tony Chrestman, head of trucking at Ruan Transportation Management, said, "Previously, I would never have thought about anyone taking one of our loads of propane and running it into a building. There's got to be improvements to background checks."[7]

Such concerns appear well founded. According to a May 2002 report by the federal Department of Transportation, suspected fraud in testing and licensing commercial drivers has been identified in sixteen states. One chief concern is that terrorists could fraudulently receive a commercial driver's license and proceed to use large trucks as weapons. Government officials worked to remove the potential for abuses in commercial licensing, but conceded that monitoring fifty separate licensing entities was an enormously difficult task.

The government is likewise concerned about potential terrorist attacks on other elements of ground transportation in the United States, including infrastructure such as bridges and tunnels. Law enforcement officials increased security at key bridges and tunnels in some cities, and implemented checkpoints to investigate vehicles before they crossed these bridges or entered some tunnels. Officials hoped to reduce the chance that a terrorist would detonate an explosive on such key transit sites, causing mass casualties and snarling the transportation system for months. However, a city's—and the nation's—transportation system is so vast and easily accessible that it was considered an impossibility to safeguard everything.

Officials also worry about how to protect the nation's public transportation system. Buses and subway systems are particularly vulnerable to attack by terrorists with conventional bombs, as attacks in other countries have demonstrated, because such transportation systems are designed to be easily accessible. For example, Palestinian suicide bombers have often blown up buses in Israel, even though that country has instituted strict and widespread security measures. The Irish

Republican Army frequently exploded bombs in the London Underground, the city's subway system, and on passenger trains. In 1995, a Japanese terrorist group called Aum Shinrikyo released sarin gas in the Tokyo subway system, an attack that killed twelve people and sent thousands to hospitals.

Beyond increasing the presence of law enforcement officials in such systems, there appeared to be little the government could do to further safeguard public transportation systems from a determined terrorist attack. Amtrak, the national passenger rail service in the United States, has instituted a few new measures to protect its system, such as limiting passengers to two pieces of carry-on luggage and routine screening of all luggage. However, such requirements would be unlikely to deter a suicide bomber. Officials hope that police and other law enforcement agencies, such as the FBI, will be able to apprehend these terrorists before they strike.

Protecting the Nation's Ports

Another worry spot for U.S. officials is the nation's seaports. Usually large, sprawling, and extremely busy, the ports are inviting targets for terrorists. More than seven thousand ships from around the world visit U.S. ports more than fifty thousand times a year, carrying more than 1 billion tons of goods. Consequently, an attack on any of the nation's one hundred major ports could severely cripple the economy. Moreover, the sheer volume of goods funneled through the nation's ports itself provides terrorists with ample opportunity to smuggle weapons, or themselves, into the country.

To help police the ports and prevent acts of terrorism, the U.S. Coast Guard now spends more than 50 percent of its time and effort on port security, up from the 1 to 2 percent prior to the 2001 terrorist attacks. The Coast Guard now puts sea marshals on ships as they enter ports, in order to prevent a terrorist hijacking. The guard also requires ships to

A reservist in the Coast Guard keeps a close watch on New York City from the East River. Terrorist attacks on U.S. ports could severely cripple the nation's economy.

notify ports about their cargoes and crews ninety-six hours in advance of arriving, allowing agents to target some ships for heightened inspection. Helping the Coast Guard, customs agents screen more cargo than they did in the past and use X-ray and other machines to ensure that items and people are not smuggled into the United States. Customs officials also require ships to document what cargo they are carrying twenty-four hours prior to leaving a foreign port.

While the added safeguards represent an improvement in security, some analysts worry that far more needs to be done to protect against a catastrophic attack. In December 2001, Senator Charles E. Schumer of New York warned:

> Our ports are a gaping hole in our national security. Terrorists have every opportunity to import and stash weapons of mass destruction—whether chemical, nuclear

or biological—in shipping containers and in port's vast cargo areas and we're not doing nearly enough about it. One ship can carry thousands of truck sized containers filled with hazardous materials. Sixty eight nuclear power plants alone are located along U.S. waterways. Protecting ourselves means protecting our ports. It's that simple.[8]

Congress later approved funding to help ports improve security. It provided money for, among other things, small boats, cameras, and vessel-tracking devices. However, given the large size of the nation's ports and the number of ports nationwide, few believed the ports could be completely protected from terrorists.

Many Americans applauded the government's steps to improve security in the nation's transportation system. Moreover, they expressed relief that the government was doing what it could to safeguard property and lives from terrorist attacks. At the same time, others worried that complete protection from terrorism was impossible. The sheer size of the United States and its enormous transportation system make it impossible, and impractical, to make the entire transportation system terrorism-proof. Although many steps have been taken, officials continue to seek more effective means of protecting the nation's transportation system from harm.

Chapter Two

Bracing for Biological, Chemical, and Nuclear Terror

O ne of the chief lessons learned after September 11, 2001, was that the nation had entered an era in which it had to expect the unexpected. Prior to the terrorist attacks, most analysts never would have dreamed that passenger jets would be hijacked and used as missiles against domestic targets. Once the shock had subsided, however, it became clear to many government and private security experts that a number of unpalatable terrorist scenarios would need to be considered in order to defend against another unthinkable attack.

As they studied the possibilities, analysts and security experts became increasingly concerned about the possibility that terrorists might try to use biological, chemical, radiological, or even nuclear devices in attacks against the United States. While the use of conventional weapons, such as bombs and other explosive devices, remained among the most obvious concerns for the nation's doomsday theorists, they reasoned that a terrorist attack utilizing weapons of mass destruction was a distinct and growing possibility. First of all, with the exception of nuclear bombs, ingredients for such weapons are relatively inexpensive. Second, they are easy to disperse and deadly. Finally, analysts worried that the raw materials for such weapons were frighteningly easy for terrorists to obtain. After the September 11 attacks, officials spent considerable time and effort deciding how to respond to the growing potential of such a threat.

Biological Weapons

Biological weapons are relatively simple and potentially disastrous. They are made by concentrating large amounts of deadly germs or viruses. Among the most serious are the bacteria that cause anthrax, botulism, plague, smallpox, and hemorrhagic fever viruses. The use of biological agents as weapons would prove particularly problematic because the germs are not visible to the naked eye and are difficult to detect without proper equipment. Large numbers of Americans could become infected with the germs before anyone realized that an attack had been made.

Because germs are naturally occurring organisms, they represent a cheap and easily accessible means for terrorists to inflict widespread casualties. In many cases, determined terrorists could harvest their own crop of deadly germs or simply find them in nature. Anthrax, for example, an infectious disease, occurs most frequently in wild and domesticated animals, such as cattle, sheep, and goats. Anthrax is common in agricultural regions in less-developed countries, the very sorts of areas where officials believe terrorist groups draw much of their support. Anthrax spores can be collected, ground into a

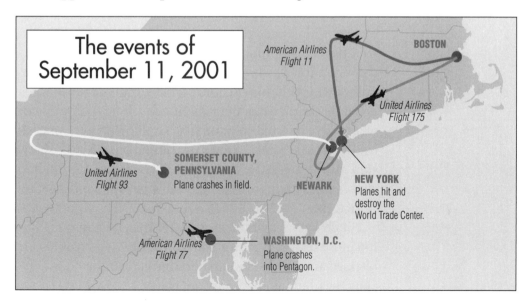

fine powder, and used as a weapon of mass destruction. Likewise, plague is a disease caused by a bacterium found in rodents and their fleas. Because it occurs naturally, terrorists could isolate a small amount of the bacterium, grow large quantities in laboratories, and use it to make deadly weapons.

Even if terrorist groups were incapable of developing their own bioweapons, government officials are concerned that terrorists could easily obtain them or the knowledge to build them. Most of these fears stem from a lack of information regarding the whereabouts of materials of the former Soviet Union's massive bioweapons program. When the Soviet empire collapsed, U.S. officials worried that bioweapons, materials to make them, and documents outlining how to make them were not secured. The officials' chief concern was that these items were obtained by terrorists or by governments sympathetic to terrorist groups. Once terrorists possess biological weapons, the weapons theoretically could be easily dispersed. For example, terrorists armed with a simple crop duster—a plane used to spray pesticides on crops—could spread vast amounts of germs into the atmosphere. In the 1960s, the U.S. Army and the Central Intelligence Agency conducted tests in the New York City subway system that dramatically illustrated the effectiveness of even primitive distribution of weaponized germs. Attempting to evaluate the consequences of a biological attack, testers dropped lightbulbs filled with microscopic particles into the subway system. They learned that the same attack using a deadly disease would have infected an estimated 3 million people. Analysts hypothesized that wind currents caused by moving subway cars could spread the germs through subway stations and ventilation systems to aboveground streets and infect scores of victims.

Such attacks would not be foolproof, however. The Japanese terrorist group, Aum Shinrikyo, in recent years released anthrax spores and botulinum toxins in Tokyo several times, but the attacks are not believed to have caused any casualties. Many bioweapons agents lose their potency when exposed to air, light, or moisture, and for this reason are actually quite difficult to turn into successful weapons.

However, even limited distribution can have serious health repercussions and cause widespread disruptions in daily lives. For example, four letters mailed in the United States in the fall of 2001 contained powdered anthrax spores, which infected twenty-three people, killed five, and made countless Americans fear the contents of their mailboxes. Contamination from those four letters closed down a U.S. Senate office building and several U.S. Postal Service installations. The incident made officials more aware than ever that terrorists could conceiveably use any means to deliver deadly germs to a broad spectrum of Americans.

Smallpox

Perhaps the most frightening prospect for security experts and government officials is the possibility that terrorists could create weapons using deadly contagious diseases, such as smallpox. Even if such weapons reached only a limited number of people, subsequent person-to-person contamination could be disastrous.

Although smallpox was officially declared eradicated by the World Health Organization in 1979, it is still among the most feared of contagious diseases because it is often lethal, always disfiguring, highly contagious, and there is no specific treatment or cure. Victims initially break out in a rash, then develop painful blisters that eventually scab and leave deep scars. Studies done in Europe before the disease was eradicated showed that a single smallpox victim had the potential to infect up to thirty people in an ever-widening ripple effect. However, infection rates would probably be much higher today because a generation of Americans has not been vaccinated against the disease. While most Americans are unfamiliar with the devastation the disease can cause, it historically has been one of the most feared of contagious illnesses. In

1947, a single case of smallpox in New York City led to the immunization of more than 6 million Americans, including then-president Harry S. Truman.

After smallpox was declared eradicated as a naturally occurring disease, the United States and the Soviet Union stored smallpox samples for research purposes. It is not known whether other nations saved samples, but there are concerns that, should terrorists gain access to the virus, they could easily wreak widespread havoc.

Agents in hazardous material protection suits decontaminate each other after inspecting a building for anthrax.

A new generation of Americans slowly began to understand the horror of a smallpox outbreak after a war game called Dark Winter was conducted by a variety of research centers. Dark Winter was a thirteen-day simulation based on the premise that terrorists had used smallpox to attack three states. The exercise clearly showed the tragic consequences of a terrorist attack using the smallpox virus. Within three weeks of the initial simulated attacks, the exercise projected that roughly three hundred thousand Americans would become infected and that one hundred thousand of those would die. By then the disease would have spread to twenty-five states and fifteen countries. In addition to death and panic, the simulation showed that Americans would have lost confidence in the government's ability to protect them. Moreover, such a crisis would have overwhelmed the nation's health care system and paralyzed the world's economy.

Preparing for the Worst

Doomsday scenarios like the one outlined by Dark Winter prompted the government to action. In December 2002, the Bush administration launched a plan to inoculate roughly 10 million health care, emergency, law enforcement, and military personnel against smallpox. The administration reasoned that people in those jobs would be frontline responders to a smallpox attack and would thus need protection from the disease. Under the administration's plan, the smallpox vaccine would be available to the general public beginning in 2004. The Department of Health and Human Services (HHS) said in 2003 it had accumulated enough smallpox vaccine to vaccinate every person in the country, should the need arise.

In addition to its inoculation initiative, HHS also began working with state and local governments to form smallpox response teams charged with providing health care services to Americans in the event of a smallpox attack. Government officials also pondered steps to contain the spread of smallpox in the event of an outbreak. Among other things, the government considered the possibility of imposing quarantines on neighborhoods and cities affected by the disease. As part of its multipronged preparation for a possible bioweapons attack, the government has prepared millions of what it calls "push packs." The kits include antibiotics, antidotes, and other drugs for use in the event of a bioterrorist attack.

Even though analysts are divided on the likelihood of terrorists using bioweapons against the United States, the Bush administration decided it would be a mistake not to act. In his 2003 State of the Union address, President Bush proposed an increase of $6 billion for research and development of vaccines to combat an array of biological threats. The plan,

Firefighters help volunteers exit a decontamination tent at a Miami stadium during a biological terrorism drill.

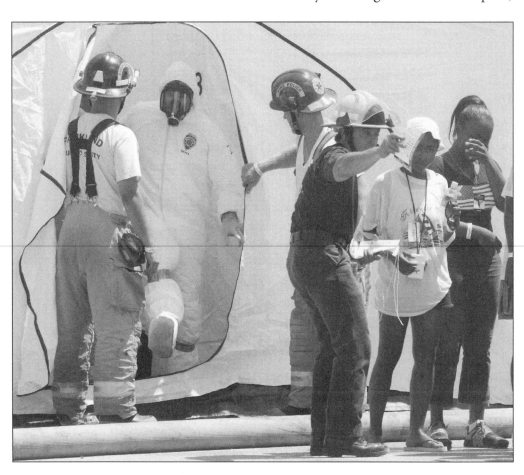

An army medic inspects the arm of a soldier who received the smallpox vaccination.

Project BioShield, was aimed at stimulating research and pro-
duction of bioterrorism defenses, primarily vaccines. Dr.
Gregory Poland, a vaccinologist at the Mayo Clinic in
Rochester, Minnesota, said the program was long overdue:
"As the might of the U.S. increases and the poverty of other
nations increases . . . what weapon do they have to strike back
with? The only one they can afford and the only one we might
not be protected against are biological weapons."[9]

The administration in January 2003 also created a system to detect the release of biological agents into the atmosphere. By adding sensors to air-quality stations already in

place and administered by the Environmental Protection Agency (EPA), the administration believed it might be possible to get early warnings if germs had been released into the environment. The EPA has approximately three thousand air-monitoring stations nationally. The units were put into place to ensure compliance with the Clean Air Act, and they provided a perfect platform for the new germ-detection units. Critics, however, warned that the detection units would not prevent an attack and that large numbers of Americans could be exposed to deadly germs before the sensors indicated a problem.

Biological weapons are feared in large measure because they occur naturally in nature and would be relatively easy for determined terrorists to gain access to. However, other

Protective suits like those pictured here keep rescue workers safe from biological and chemical dangers.

potential terrorist weapons are equally worrisome, including chemical, radiological, and nuclear weapons.

Chemical Dangers

Like biological weapons, chemical weapons pose vexing problems for public health officials. Toxic chemicals are inexpensive, readily available, and easy to disperse. Like bioweapons, they can cause agony and death. The sheer number of potential chemicals terrorists could use as weapons is staggering. It ranges from concoctions such as sarin gas, which was developed for use as a weapon, to simple agricultural pesticides. Consequently, officials must envision a host of unsavory scenarios in order to prepare for possible chemical attacks.

Experts say that it would be extraordinarily difficult for terrorists, working in a home lab, to fabricate an effective chemical weapon. Nevertheless, the U.S. military uncovered evidence in Afghanistan that Osama bin Laden's terrorist network was developing crude chemical devices for possible use against the United States. Moreover, a number of countries identified by the U.S. government as sponsors of terrorism are known to have made such weapons. Officials fear that these governments might offer the weapons to terrorist groups to strike at the United States. Although they do not completely discount the possibility that terrorists will develop or otherwise obtain chemical weaponry, government experts consider such scenarios relatively remote.

Instead, they believe it would be far more likely for terrorists to turn America's financial and technological superiority against itself. For example, they hypothesize that terrorists could blow up a U.S. chemical plant, an explosion that would disperse deadly gases into the air. Likewise, terrorists could explode a truck containing hazardous material. Either attack could prove extremely deadly. As one measure of the chaos such an attack could trigger, experts point to a 1984 industrial accident in Bhopal, India. A Union

President Bush holds a chemical agent detector that alerts safety workers to the presence of toxic chemicals in the air.

Carbide pesticide plant there accidentally released methyl isocyanate gas into the atmosphere. The disaster killed nearly four thousand people, about one thousand more than perished in the 2001 terrorist attacks. Perhaps even more chilling, a U.S. Army study estimated that nearly 2.5 million people could die if terrorists were successful in blowing up a chemical plant, sending clouds of deadly gases over an American city.

With protection in mind, the federal government provided the nation's 120 largest cities with millions of dollars to train and conduct exercises to prepare for chemical attacks. Current disaster plans call for police officers, firefighters, and paramedics to be the first to respond to a chemical calamity. They would be responsible for decontaminating victims and treating them with appropriate antidotes. These officials would also establish decontamination zones and treatment areas. Once victims had received initial care, they would be sent to hospitals for further treatment.

Some critics question whether such a response would be adequate in the face of a concerted terrorist attack. They especially worry that the nation's health care system could become

During a practice drill, hazardous materials workers decontaminate each other. Millions of dollars have been spent to conduct terrorism drills.

overwhelmed by the sheer numbers of victims. The availability of enough hospital beds to accommodate mass casualties is a primary concern. Analysts point to the 1995 terrorist attack in the Tokyo, Japan, subway system as a telling example. Roughly four thousand people who were not exposed to the sarin gas nevertheless rushed to hospitals. The crush of people overwhelmed Tokyo's hospital facilities, inhibiting doctors' ability to treat those who actually had been exposed to the deadly gas. These scenarios and others will have to be considered as officials make contingency plans for disaster.

Radioactive Weapons

Another potential concern for the nation's preparedness planners is the possibility that terrorists could use radiation as a weapon. Radiation, a form of energy emitted from the nuclei of atoms, is extremely harmful to humans. Although people are exposed to radiation every day from a variety of naturally occurring sources, large amounts of radiation can cause sickness and death. Symptoms of radiation sickness range from vomiting to internal hemorrhaging. Exposure to radiation also can increase the risk of certain types of cancer.

Government fears about the potential for terrorists to attempt a radiation attack on Americans only increased when officials in 2002 arrested an alleged al-Qaeda terrorist who they claim had plotted to build and detonate a so-called dirty bomb. Dirty bombs are conventional bombs that have been laced with radioactive material. Such a weapon could disperse radiation into the air. In turn, people would breathe it or absorb it through their skin.

In order to build a dirty bomb, however, terrorists would first have to obtain radioactive materials. Although the government has increased efforts to limit international trafficking in radioactive materials, officials conceded it would be impossible to completely eliminate clandestine sales of the materials. Fearful that terrorists might already have access to radioactive materials, the government installed radiation detectors at a number of locations throughout the nation. Such areas included airports, seaports, and highways. The sensors could help officials detect the presence of dirty bombs or the raw material used to build them.

Nuclear Terror

As frightening as the prospect of a radiation attack can be, officials have been forced to confront an even scarier possibility: Terrorists could develop or obtain a nuclear weapon. Government officials believe it unlikely to happen. However, they recognize that the consequences of terrorists armed with a nuclear bomb are so hideous that it would be foolhardy to completely discount the possibility. Some experts believe a small group of as few as four scientists could build a rudimentary nuclear bomb, assuming they could obtain the necessary enriched uranium.

Analysts also believe it is possible for terrorist groups to steal or obtain small battlefield nuclear weapons. Even a relatively small, one-kiloton, nuclear bomb has the explosive power of a thousand tons of TNT. Doomsday theorists estimate that the explosion of such a bomb in midtown Manhattan could kill more than two hundred thousand people and injure another two hundred thousand. The blast would also obliterate structures within a wide radius and would produce enough radioactive fallout within three miles of the detonation to kill half of the people exposed to the radiation within a few weeks. Larger nuclear weapons, of course, would have an even more devastating impact.

While the use of nuclear weapons has been a threat for many years, their use would be particularly dangerous in the hands of terrorists. For example, terrorists would be more than likely to target a large urban area in order to inflict the most physical and psychological damage, and would not limit themselves to a military target. Moreover, terrorists more than likely would be willing to die in the process of setting off such a weapon, as many are religious fanatics driven by

South Koreans protest North Korean leader Kim Jong il's nuclear program. North Korea's nuclear program is a growing concern to national security.

the ideal of martyrdom. (Martyrs are those willing to die in defense of their beliefs.) Finally, terrorists are not tied to any particular state. Because they are far-flung, shadowy collections of individuals, it would be difficult for the government to seek reprisal.

The primary government response to the risk of a potential nuclear attack rests in attempting to make it less likely that such an attack ever occurs. The government has worked with Russia to secure existing nuclear weapons, along with supplies of plutonium and the enriched uranium necessary to construct a nuclear weapon. The government has also beefed up intelligence programs to monitor potential nuclear threats.

Responding to a Crisis

In the event of a nuclear attack, the government has in place plans to deal with the resulting crisis. Police, firefighters, and medical personnel would be charged with decontaminating victims and taking them to hospitals away from the blast zone. At the same time, the Energy Department's Nuclear Emergency Search Team and other federal agencies with specialists in nuclear decontamination would respond to the crisis. The challenges facing municipal and federal government officials would be daunting. In addition to sealing off radioactive areas, officials would need to provide food, water, and shelter for those displaced by the blast. They also would have to set up communication centers and medical facilities.

In the event that terrorists are unable to build a nuclear bomb, government officials worry that they might try to sabotage a nuclear power plant. The Bush administration therefore ordered increased security at the nation's nuclear facilities. Even a marginally successful attack against one facility could cause far-reaching health problems. Anyone near the plant would have to immediately begin taking potassium iodide to protect against thyroid cancer. Following the September 11 attacks, the government stockpiled 1.6 million doses of potassium iodide, though such numbers could be woefully inadequate if terrorists were successful in seriously damaging a nuclear plant.

Although it is difficult to imagine a scenario in which biological, chemical, radiological, or nuclear weapons are used against U.S. citizens, the 2001 terrorist attacks emphatically drove home the need for the United States to be vigilant and prepared for a variety of ghastly and previously unthinkable blows. Moreover, the government needed to consider such possibilities in order to improve its capabilities to prevent such calamities from ever occurring. Unless analysts gave thought to the different ways in which terrorists might be able to strike at and undermine society, officials would be unable to improve security. However, the country's sheer size and openness made preparing for the unthinkable a daunting task of enormous scope.

Chapter Three

Racial Profiling and the Battle Against Terrorism

As the government took steps to determine the identities of those who perpetrated the September 11 attacks, it undertook a nationwide dragnet to find accomplices and forestall a possible second wave of assaults. Investigators quickly learned that the nineteen hijackers reponsible for the tragedy all were young Middle Eastern males and followers of Islam. Those simple facts became overriding considerations in the government's reaction to the attacks and drove the continuing investigation.

The nation's fight against terror suddenly landed Americans in the middle of a national debate about racial profiling. Racial profiling is a practice in which law enforcement officials use race as a factor in deciding whether to target individuals for investigation. Some in government contend that the government has never engaged in the practice. In fact, Robert S. Mueller III, director of the FBI, said his agents explicitly have been told not to use racial profiling as they decide whether to conduct investigations of terror suspects. To others, however, it seemed clear that by focusing investigations and suspicion on Middle Easterners, the government was violating cherished American ideals of fairness and justice, and fanning flames of prejudice in the process. Still others believed that the use of racial profiling helped the government use its limited law enforcement resources more wisely and effectively. Whether they liked it or not, Americans found themselves walking a tightrope between granting civil liberties and protecting the nation as a whole.

Government Focus on Middle Eastern Males

Based in large measure on what it had learned about the hijackers, the government detained thousands of Middle

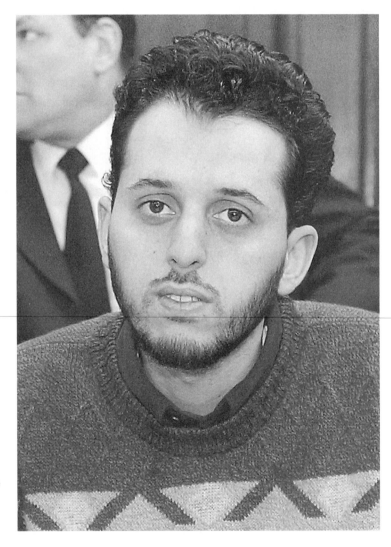

Mounir al-Motassadeq was arrested in connection with the September 11 terrorist attacks on the basis of flimsy evidence. Al-Motassadeq is one of the thousands of Middle Eastern men who have been detained because of racial profiling.

50

Eastern and Islamic males, as well as American-born Muslims and males of Middle Eastern ancestry, for questioning. Initially, one thousand Middle Eastern males were detained and four thousand subpoenas for others were issued as part of a nationwide search for terrorists. Attorney General John Ashcroft also requested so-called voluntary questioning of another five thousand Middle Eastern men in November 2001. By 2003, the government had obtained eighteen thousand subpoenas and search warrants in its attempt to prevent further terrorist attacks, and each was driven by the government's profile of the September 11 hijackers.

Even more people were detained when the United States went to war against Iraq in 2003. The FBI interviewed an estimated five thousand to eleven thousand Iraqis living in the United States in an attempt to discover if the Iraqi government had plotted retaliatory terrorist attacks against the United States. A number of Iraqis were arrested as the war began, with the government focusing on people thought to "pose a threat to the safety and security of the American people,"[10] according to a spokesman with the Department of Homeland Security.

This focus on Iraqi Americans was controversial because it highlighted tensions about racial profiling. Some argued that it was unfair, and ironic, to target Iraqis who had come to the United States in large part to escape a totalitarian government. Others said it would be foolhardy not to, arguing that even a handful of terrorists intending to use an attack to become Iraqi heroes could jeopardize the safety of millions of Americans.

Most of the suspects detained by the government were held indefinitely and not formally charged with crimes, as officials attempted to untangle the guilty from the innocent. Eventually some of those being held were found innocent of terrorism but guilty of visa violations. Other Middle Eastern men held by the government were eventually deported after secret hearings, and Americans may never learn why the men were forced to leave the country. An antiterrorism law passed prior to the September 11 tragedy allows the government to use evidence that defendants are unaware of—and thus cannot challenge—to detain and deport immigrants suspected of terrorism. The law has since been used almost exclusively in the cases of Middle Eastern and Muslim immigrants, and by 2003, close to five hundred Middle Eastern Muslim men had been deported from the United States.

Although the government said that the manhunt, which focused on Middle Eastern males, uncovered a number of terrorists, others worried that the civil rights of a vast number of people of Middle Eastern ancestry had been violated. They believed that many of those held by the government were innocent of any wrongdoing, guilty only of being Middle Eastern males at a time when many Americans simplistically viewed them as potential terrorists.

Government Successes

Despite growing unease among many civil libertarians, the government uncovered a number of would-be terrorists and terrorist cells, that is, small groups of terrorists established to undertake missions against the United States. All were the result of the government's strategy of focusing on Middle Eastern and Muslim males in the United States. By early 2003, the government had brought 211 criminal charges against men of Middle Eastern ancestry on suspicion of terrorism and obtained 108 convictions or guilty pleas.

The government also had broken up four alleged terrorist rings in Buffalo, New York; Detroit, Michigan; Seattle, Washington; and Portland, Oregon. The government's focus on Muslim men and those of Middle Eastern ancestry appeared to help the government to forestall future terrorist attacks. Although some of those arrested were eventually found innocent of terrorism, many Americans believed the government was justified in focusing its antiterrorism campaign on Middle Eastern men.

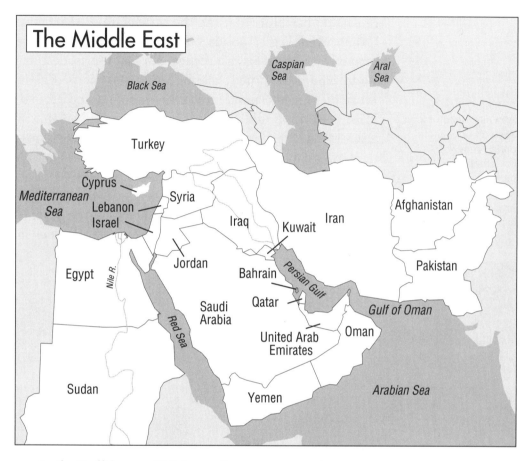

The Middle East

Aral Sea

Caspian Sea

Black Sea

Turkey

Cyprus

Mediterranean Sea

Lebanon

Israel

Syria

Iraq

Kuwait

Iran

Afghanistan

Jordan

Egypt

Nile R.

Bahrain

Persian Gulf

Qatar

Saudi Arabia

Red Sea

United Arab Emirates

Gulf of Oman

Oman

Pakistan

Arabian Sea

Sudan

Yemen

In the Buffalo case, U.S. law enforcement agencies arrested five U.S. citizens on charges of providing support to the al-Qaeda terrorist network. The government said Faysal Galab, Sahim A. Alwan, Yahya A. Goba, Shafel Mosed, and Yasein Taher, American-born residents of Lackawanna, New York, had undergone weapons training at an al-Qaeda camp in Afghanistan. In announcing the arrests of the men, Deputy Attorney General Larry Thompson said the Justice Department would "aggressively pursue terrorists and those who aid terrorists, wherever they reside."[11]

The Detroit case featured four men who were charged with planning terrorist attacks against the United States. Among the items found in their possession was a videotape that authorities believed was a surveillance tape of Disneyland, in Anaheim, California, and the MGM Grand Hotel and Casino, in Las Vegas, Nevada. Officials believed the men were planning an attack against the two popular tourist destinations. The government claimed that the men—Karim Koubriti, Ahmed Hanna, Farouk Ali-Haimoud, and a fourth identified only as Abdella—also planned to conduct attacks against the U.S. air base in Incirlik, Turkey, and against a hospital in Jordan. The men allegedly belonged to an Algerian terrorist group that had financial ties to al-Qaeda.

The Portland and Seattle cases likewise involved men of Middle Eastern ancestry. In the Portland case, the government charged six people with belonging to a terrorist cell that

Attorney General John Ashcroft announces during a news conference that hundreds of people have been detained for immigration violations, including suspected al-Qaeda members.

attempted to join al-Qaeda and Taliban forces fighting in Afghanistan against the United States. And finally, the government in the Seattle case charged that Ernest James Ujaama and several other U.S. residents had conspired to provide support to terrorists.

Middle Eastern men and other immigrants line up outside an Immigration and Naturalization Service office to register with the U.S. government.

Registration Programs

In further efforts to prevent another round of terrorist attacks the government instituted a special registration procedure for some of the 35 million people who enter the United States from other countries annually to work, study, or travel. Focusing almost exclusively on men entering the country from Middle Eastern nations, the government believed the registration program would help keep better track of foreigners within the United States and make it more difficult

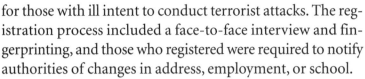

for those with ill intent to conduct terrorist attacks. The registration process included a face-to-face interview and fingerprinting, and those who registered were required to notify authorities of changes in address, employment, or school.

The registration requirement applied to males entering the country from Egypt, Jordan, Kuwait, Pakistan, Saudi Arabia, Afghanistan, Algeria, Bahrain, Eritrea, Lebanon, Morocco, Oman, Qatar, Somalia, Tunisia, United Arab Emirates, Yemen, Iran, Libya, Sudan, and Syria. The registration requirement also applied to predominantly Muslim Indonesia and Bangladesh, as well as to North Korea. By focusing on men from these nations, the government assumed that it would be able to more precisely identify any would-be terrorists.

At the same time, in 2003, a new computerized system called SEVIS (Student and Exchange Visitor Information System) was launched to enable the federal government to better monitor foreign students. The idea behind the system is to reveal whether foreigners who receive student visas actually show up at school and remain there. Tracking foreign students is now a priority because a number of the September 11 hijackers had either overstayed or otherwise violated provisions of their student visas. Although all foreign national students are to be tracked by the system, students from Middle Eastern nations are of particular concern to government immigration officials. For example, the government is unlikely to devote many resources to finding a Swiss national who overstays a student visa but likely will devote considerable energy and time in tracking down a similar Egyptian national.

In announcing implementation of the system, a Justice Department press release said that SEVIS "demonstrates the commitment of the [government] to develop a system by which our country can invite international students and exchange visitors to enjoy an educational experience in the United States, but also protect our nation's security by maintaining accurate records on who is inside our borders."[12] However, critics of the registration and tracking systems complain that the systems unfairly single out Middle Eastern and Muslim men for heightened scrutiny. They argue that each person should be judged on his own merits, not viewed with suspicion simply because he comes from the Middle East or is a practicing Muslim. They also argue that the systems are riddled with problems and are unlikely to significantly enhance national security.

On the other hand, proponents of the system argue that, because of the backgrounds of the September 11 terrorists, it only makes sense that the government spend more time scrutinizing those from the Middle East. Advocates also argue that the systems already have helped the government identify and monitor terrorists within the United States. In early 2003, Attorney General Ashcroft told Congress, "Hundreds and hundreds of suspected terrorists have been identified and tracked throughout the United States"[13] as a result of the new registration programs.

The Council of Arab-American Organizations (prominent members pictured) is one of the most vocal critics of the immigrant registration program.

Activists in India show their support for the U.S. government's decision to freeze the assets of suspected terrorist organizations.

Following the Money Trail

In addition to trying to ferret out terrorists before they strike against U.S. interests, the government has attempted to squash the flow of money to terrorist groups by targeting Muslim charities and businesses owned by people of Middle Eastern descent. On September 24, 2001, President Bush signed Executive Order 13224 to freeze the assets of terrorists or those who seek to finance them. By 2003, the executive order had been used to freeze $124 million in assets in more than six hundred accounts globally. The government also launched seventy investigations into terrorist financing, focusing on Muslim and Middle Eastern charities, businesses, and individuals. Those investigations led to twenty convictions and guilty pleas.

The government also expanded its efforts globally to prevent terrorists from both hatching plots against the United States and financing them in far reaches of the world. The effort focused almost exclusively on Middle Eastern Muslims, including the case of two Yemeni citizens who the FBI arrested on charges of conspiring to provide money to terrorists. The government charged that the Yemeni men provided bin Laden with $20 million in financing.

The focus on Islamic charities and institutions has launched another debate regarding the targeting of American Muslims in the war on terror. In some cases, relying on ethnicity and religion has allowed the government to seize funds that might have helped finance attacks against the United States. In others, however, it has led to the interrogation of innocent people simply because of their links to Islam or the Middle East. Rita Katz, a terrorism expert in Washington, D.C., says the government is being practical. "A rich Saudi who wants to fund radical ideas or terrorists like Hamas and al Qaeda knows he can't send the money directly so he filters it through companies and charities, often in the U.S. or Europe."[14] Others, however, like Nancy Luque, a Washington attorney who represents many of the charities that have been raided, calls the government's campaign, nicknamed Operation Green Quest, "a smearing."[15] Americans like Luque fear the government has unfairly targeted Muslim institutions by casting a wide, blind net in its search for terrorists.

Backlash and Debate

Given the ethnicities of the September 11 hijackers and the government's subsequent focus on Middle Eastern Muslims in its declared war against terrorism, many Americans vented their frustrations with overt hostility to anyone of Middle Eastern descent. Some angry Americans resorted to hate crimes, graffiti, and plain prejudice in the weeks and months following the attacks. Such reactions even extended to members of Congress. Representative John Cooksey, a Louisiana Republican, said, "If I see someone [who] comes in that's got a diaper on his head and a fan belt wrapped around the diaper on his head, that guy needs to be pulled over."[16]

As ugly as Cooksey's sentiment was to Middle Eastern and Muslim Americans, these citizens faced the even uglier, more dangerous threat of physical harm. For example, Charles D. Franklin was charged on March 28, 2002, with driving his truck into the door of the Islamic Center Mosque in Tallahassee, Florida, in an apparent attempt at revenge for the terrorist attacks. In Arizona, a Sikh gas station owner was shot and killed by a man whose only rationale for the violence was the simple declaration, "I am an American."[17]

Some Americans advocated putting Middle Easterners into internment camps, as both a means of protecting Middle Easterners from harm and ensuring that they could not conduct future attacks against the United States. The idea for such camps invokes memories of World War II, when the government put 120,000 Japanese Americans in internment camps in one of the nation's most discredited acts. Other reactions to the 2001 attacks were more subdued but nevertheless raised concerns about racial profiling and prejudice. For example, a week after the attacks, the passengers and crew of a Northwest Airlines flight asked three men of Middle Eastern descent to get off an airplane prior to takeoff, fearful that the trio might be intent upon hijacking the plane.

The government itself appeared to send a mixed message. On the one hand, government law enforcement officials were thoroughly investigating and questioning Muslim and Middle Eastern men exclusively in its search for potential terrorists. At the same time, it was vigorously pursuing hate crimes perpetrated against Middle Easterners and Muslims. By early

2003, the Justice Department's Civil Rights Division had investigated nearly four hundred cases of alleged violence or threats against Arabs, Muslims, Sikhs, and others. The government enthusiastically prosecuted a number of cases of violence or threatened violence, including a case in which Zachary J. Rolnik threatened to kill James J. Zogby, president of the Arab American Institute. On June 6, 2002, Rolnik pleaded guilty.

Anti-Arab insults and vandalism of his San Francisco shop have convinced this Jordanian man to return to his home country.

Officials Decry Profiling

To an extent, the government's sensitivities to the concerns of the nation's Middle Eastern community were well received. Zogby said many Arab Americans felt the government had taken the steps necessary to make them feel safe in a potentially hostile environment. Zogby told a journalist, "The Justice Department has been in touch with us every day. We've never seen a response like this. The community feels like the FBI is trying to protect them."[18]

Other people of Middle Eastern descent were partially calmed by the actions of other government officials, who flatly rejected proposals for policies that would subject Muslims and Middle Easterners to heightened scrutiny. For example, the Department of Transportation rejected an idea to impose tougher security restrictions on all Muslims and people of Middle Eastern descent at the nation's airports. On April 20, 2002, Transportation Secretary Norman Y. Mineta said such a policy would provide only a false sense of security. He noted, for example, that a seventy-year-old man and a twenty-five-year-old woman posing as father and daughter exploded a bomb on a flight from Baghdad to Thailand in 1987. Neither of the perpetrators were Middle Eastern. "Racial profiling . . . cannot provide us with the security that we need,"[19] Mineta said.

Some members of Congress tried to use their positions to calm the passions of Americans angered by the terrorist attacks, urging them not to indiscriminately assume the worst about Middle Easterners. On October 1, 2001, for example, Senator Russell Feingold, a Wisconsin Democrat, and Representative John Conyers Jr., a Michigan Democrat, wrote a letter to the heads of the nation's major airlines. In it, they asked that airlines not discriminate against Muslims and those of Middle Eastern ancestry. In their letter, the lawmakers said, "The American people are understandably feeling anxious about returning to our nation's skies, but we should not give the terrorists a victory by allowing the erosion of fundamental civil rights. All Americans have the same right to travel free of discrimination."[20]

"Americans Must Treat Each Other with Respect"

Some government officials consistently urged Americans not to lash out at those of Middle Eastern descent. In a September 26, 2001, meeting with Muslim leaders, President Bush attempted to make clear that the government was interested solely in apprehending terrorists and not in terrorizing

Muslims or Middle Easterners. In an earlier speech on September 17, 2001, Bush spoke at the Islamic Center in Washington, D.C., where he said:

Four friends sit together between classes at a Michigan high school where 90 percent of the student body is Muslim.

> America counts millions of Muslims amongst our citizens, and Muslims make an incredibly valuable contribution in our country. Muslims are doctors, lawyers, law professors, members of the military, entrepreneurs, shopkeepers, moms, and dads. And they need to be treated with respect. In our anger and emotion, our fellow Americans must treat each other with respect.[21]

Bush's call for respect, however, seemed inconsistent to some Muslims and Middle Easterners, who believed the government's focus on antiterrorism unfairly singled them out for scrutiny. Yahya Basha, president of the American Muslim Council, tried to be sympathetic to the government's position when he said: "I understand that civil liberties may be off the agenda for now, until we all feel safe and secure; we don't want to stand in the way of national security. But we ask for a reasonable balance between protecting our country and civil liberties."[22]

Even as the debate over racial profiling swirled, the use of profiling appeared to be a potent tool for law enforcement officials. By focusing on Muslims and people of Middle Eastern descent, the government was able to arrest, detain, deport, or track individuals identified as terrorists or potential terrorists. However, the government's approach appeared to many to call into question cherished American rights, such as the one that says people are presumed innocent until proven guilty. The government found itself in the precarious position of attempting to balance the sometimes diametrically opposed goals of promoting civil liberties for all and protecting the nation from attacks by shadowy international terrorist organizations. As the nation's war against terrorism continued, so did the national debate over the propriety and existence of racial profiling.

Chapter Four

A Consolidation of Power

In the immediate aftermath of the 2001 terrorist attacks, the U.S. government quickly moved to minimize the risk of further assaults and to search for ways to better equip the government to handle future threats. The U.S. Congress was particularly active. In a flurry of activity following September 11, Congress approved sweeping laws to reorganize the government to make it more responsive to the threats of terrorism and to significantly enhance law enforcement tools to make it easier for the government to find, track, and arrest would-be terrorists. Even with the broad changes, which brought about a major consolidation of power, the government faced an enormous task in attempting to safeguard a free and open society from terrorist attacks.

Homeland Security Department

One major way the government hoped to better position itself to analyze terrorist threats, act upon them, and provide a rapid response should another attack occur was through a massive government reorganization. In 2002, Congress created a new cabinet-level department, the Department of Homeland Security. The move represented a major overhaul of the government—the largest government restructuring since 1947, when President Harry S. Truman merged the War and Navy Departments into the Department of Defense.

The sheer size of the restructuring was staggering. To create the new department, twenty-two existing agencies and bureaus distributed throughout the federal government were consolidated, bringing together roughly 170,000 employees. Among other things, the Homeland Security Department absorbed the Coast Guard, the Border Patrol, the Customs Service, the Secret Service, the Transportation Security Administration, and the troubled Immigration and Naturalization Service (INS). The idea behind the consolidation was that such centralization would improve the government's ability to coordinate antiterrorism efforts. Proponents also believed the restructuring would enhance the government's ability to gather and synthesize information about terrorists and their plots, while enhancing border security.

The Homeland Security Department has four primary divisions. One is responsible for strengthening and administering border and transportation security. The second is designed to ensure emergency preparedness and to oversee

A Blackhawk helicopter flies over New York City as part of the Department of Homeland Security's effort to patrol airspace.

a response to future terrorist attacks. Another is charged with developing and implementing means of protecting the public from biological, chemical, radiological, or nuclear attacks. The final division was established to create a clearinghouse for terrorism intelligence.

Tom Ridge, director of Homeland Security, discusses his mission to coordinate intelligence information from different agencies with officials from the U.S. Coast Guard.

Coordinating Information

Officials especially hoped that the restructuring would prompt improvements in border security, particularly in the way the INS was run. The service's credibility, and that of the entire federal government, was called into question on March 11, 2002, when the INS sent a letter to a Florida flight school announcing that the INS had approved visas so that two foreigners, Mohammed Atta and Marwa Al-Shehhi, were cleared to receive flight training. The two men, of course, were among the nineteen September 11 hijackers and had been dead for six months. The INS not only had let the foreign-born terrorists and their accomplices into the country, it had been unable to keep track of them.

Lawmakers crafting legislation for the Homeland Security Department attributed part of the problems at the INS to a contradictory mission. The INS had been responsible for providing immigrant services, such as granting the documents that allow immigrants to live, study, and work in the United States. At the same time, the INS was also charged with enforcing a wide variety of immigration laws, including the daunting task of inspecting every person who enters the country, conducting criminal investigations of immigrants, and patrolling the borders for illegal immigrants. As just one measure of the enormity of the immigration service's task, fewer than five thousand INS agents in 2001 had to conduct more than 510 million inspections of people arriving in the United States at more than three hundred ports of entry. Moreover, the INS had less than two thousand investigators in 2001 to find up to 8 million illegal residents in the United States.

To fix these problems, Congress added the INS to the new Homeland Security Department and separated the immigration services from the law enforcement functions of the service within the new department. Moreover, Congress approved funding for the INS to hire thousands of new Border Patrol agents and inspectors. Although critics worried that immigration services might suffer by moving the INS to the new department, advocates believed that folding the INS into the Department of Homeland Security would greatly enhance the agency's effectiveness and provide the government with an enhanced ability to track foreign visitors.

In creating the new department, lawmakers also hoped to significantly improve the government's ability to synthesize and analyze intelligence information. As officials sorted through the intelligence they had prior to September 11, many realized that the government had a significant amount of information that, if acted upon, might have prevented the terrorist attacks. The problem was not so much a lack of information as it was a lack of awareness of the significant intelligence government officials already possessed. Summing up the situation, one FBI agent said, "We didn't know what we knew."[23] Consequently, one of the divisions in the new department is responsible for culling reports from all U.S. intelligence sources. Analysts within the division assess the risks posed by any threats and issue warnings to law enforcement agencies and the public.

To keep the public informed of the likelihood of a terrorist attack at any given time, the department also developed a color-coded system based on the division's analysis of intelligence information. Under the system, a low level of threat is represented by the color green, and blue means the nation is on guarded alert. Yellow indicates an elevated threat and is issued when the government believes there is a significant chance of a terrorist attack. Orange signals a high threat level, and red points to what the government considers a severe risk of terrorist attack.

Although designed to keep the public informed about potential terrorism risks, the color-coded system has been criticized by those who believe it is meaningless to most Americans. For example, knowledge that there is a high probability of a terrorist attack is of little use to the average American, who more likely wants to know whether it is safe to go to a neighborhood shopping mall, sports venue, or to cross a bridge. By early 2003, the government had not been able to refine its warning system to pinpoint particular places that were considered likely to be attacked, and many Americans had begun to discount the government's threat assessments.

Improved Readiness Debated

When it comes to the question of how well the massive government reorganization will work and how effective it will be in combating terrorism, analysts are divided. All agree that if

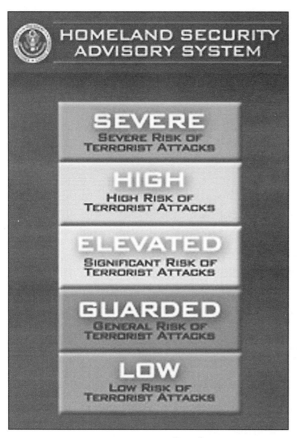

HOMELAND SECURITY ADVISORY SYSTEM

SEVERE
SEVERE RISK OF TERRORIST ATTACKS

HIGH
HIGH RISK OF TERRORIST ATTACKS

ELEVATED
SIGNIFICANT RISK OF TERRORIST ATTACKS

GUARDED
GENERAL RISK OF TERRORIST ATTACKS

LOW
LOW RISK OF TERRORIST ATTACKS

The color-coded terrorist threat system alerts Americans to the likelihood of terrorist attacks.

the department performs as intended, the government's antiterrorism efforts will be significantly streamlined. Consequently, the United States will be able to respond more quickly and effectively to perceived threats. For example, many analysts believe that by creating a centralized clearinghouse for intelligence information the government's ability to monitor and evaluate potential threats will be greatly enhanced. Skeptics, however, question whether the reorganization will actually improve domestic security. They point out that merely putting a host of disparate agencies under one roof will not necessarily enhance the government's ability to fight terrorism. Moreover, they worry that instead the move will only bog down antiterrorism efforts in bureaucracy.

One key concern among experts is that the massive reorganization, with its primary focus on domestic security, may inadvertently reduce the government's ability to carry out other important missions. As just one example, the U.S. Coast Guard has traditionally focused its efforts on conducting search-and-rescue operations at sea. With the guard's new emphasis on counterterrorism efforts, critics worry that search-and-rescue exercises could suffer—with disastrous results for distressed boaters.

Despite such concerns, government officials hailed creation of the new department as a significant step in bolstering the nation's readiness for, and defense against, future terrorist attacks. However, the department's own officials cautioned that being prepared for possible terrorist attacks is not solely a job for government agencies and emergency officials. Rather, it is a job for all Americans. The department urged Americans to be vigilant, keeping watch for signs of suspicious activity that might be related to a terrorist attack. The department also urged Americans to make sure they are adequately prepared and to formulate clear-cut plans in the event an attack is made. In an online article, the Department of Homeland Security stated:

An armed Coast Guard ship patrols the waters of Boston, Massachusetts, as part of its new counterterrorism mission.

Improving our national preparedness is not just a job for the professionals—law enforcement, firefighters and others. All Americans should begin a process of learning about potential threats so we are better prepared to react during an attack.

While there is no way to predict what will happen, or what your personal circumstances will be, there are simple things you can do now to prepare yourself and your loved ones.[24]

The Patriot Act

In addition to reorganizing the government to better position it to respond to the threat of terrorism and enlisting ordinary Americans in the fight, Congress also sought to bolster the government's ability to locate and stop potential terrorists before they struck. Following the attacks, many government officials complained that agencies responsible for promoting security were not able to adequately foresee potential threats because the nation's laws did not authorize the necessary law enforcement tools.

In the climate of fear and apprehension that followed September 11, therefore, the government sought, and Congress approved, a host of new powers for law enforcement officials. On October 26, 2001, roughly six weeks after the terrorist attacks, lawmakers approved, with little debate, one of the first major pieces of antiterrorism legislation—the USA Patriot Act. In passing the measure, members of Congress attempted to respond to the Justice Department's request for expanded intelligence-gathering powers, based on the theory that the department might have been able to unravel the September 11 plot before it had occurred, if only it had broader powers to collect information. Among other things, the department requested and received increased authority to conduct physical searches, obtain wiretaps, and engage in electronic surveillance.

Some of the changes brought about by the Patriot Act were natural extensions of powers federal agencies already had to monitor terrorism suspects. These additions were considered necessary in order to eliminate gaps in the government's ability to track terrorists as they moved around the world. For example, the Patriot Act extended the government's ability to obtain so-called roving surveillance of a person's phone activities, that is, a surveillance not tied to a single phone. Previously, the government could conduct roving surveillance only in domestic law enforcement activities. The Patriot Act gave the government the same power in foreign intelligence operations. Likewise, the law enhanced the government's authority to obtain subpoenas and search warrants to cull information from cable companies, which increasingly provided the same sorts of services as telephone and Internet service providers.

Other aspects of the Patriot Act were designed to give the government improved abilities to monitor and track suspected terrorists, who increasingly made use of computers and the Internet to communicate their plans. The new law authorized monitoring of both the source and destination of e-mail and Internet activity, a significant expansion of power that government officials said would greatly enhance efforts to track terrorists. Previous law had only allowed law enforcement officials to install what are called pen registers, which record telephone numbers dialed from a suspect's phone, and trap-and-trace devices, which record numbers from which incoming phone calls originate. The Patriot Act goes significantly further, however, by allowing use of such devices to record a suspect's Internet activities.

Such tools could prove invaluable to the government. For example, if a suspect wrote or received regular e-mail messages from other known terrorists, officials could gain important insights into terrorist organizations and methods. Moreover, if a suspect regularly visited anti-American extremist websites or sites devoted to helping people build weapons, law enforcement officials would have further grounds for continued and heightened surveillance.

Under the Patriot Act, graduate student Tomas Foral (pictured) was charged with keeping anthrax in a university research lab.

The Patriot Act also included provisions which effectively legitimized a powerful FBI software program that enables agents to read e-mail transmissions. Originally called Carnivore and now known by the less descriptive name, DCS 1000, the software program is a powerful tool that could the-oretically allow authorities to uncover terrorist plans. Capturing the content of e-mail messages is considered a search subject to the Constitution's Fourth Amendment, meaning the government must first obtain a warrant before reading a suspect's e-mail. However, the Patriot Act effectively sanctioned use of the program as a pen register and trap-and-trace device. This means, that under the new law, whenever the government uses its own software for such purposes, it must merely keep and provide a record of the information collected.

The Patriot Act also greatly increases the ways in which the government can collect information. The Fourth Amendment to the U.S. Constitution has required law enforcement agents to provide immediate notification when a search is being conducted. The new law, however, has broadened the circumstances under which secret searches can be conducted. This tool could help investigators gather evidence in terrorism cases as part of larger investigations

Police officers in Oregon arrest a woman who staged a protest of the Patriot Act in the middle of a busy street.

into terrorist activities. Among other things, the new law allows the government to conduct surveillance or clandestine physical searches of foreign agents, including U.S. citizens, for up to ninety days, even if the government does not have probable cause to believe a crime is being committed.

Government advocates of the expanded powers provided by the Patriot Act argue that the new law enforcement tools are necessary to allow the government to prevent another wave of terrorist attacks. Because the risks of inaction are so high and carry with them the potential for widespread death and destruction, extraordinary measures are not only appropriate, they claim, but necessary.

Civil Rights Concerns

Critics of these new powers and systems warn that what terrorists might be unable to dismantle, efforts to eradicate terrorists will. In other words, while the expanded powers could have obvious benefits for investigators seeking out terrorism leads, the new authority also holds the potential to significantly erode privacy and civil rights, cherished as one of America's greatest liberties. As critic Stephen J. Schulhofer, a New York University law professor noted, "Records pertaining to any American citizen are now available for FBI inspection on a clandestine basis whenever the agent states that the records 'are sought for an authorized investigation . . . to protect against international terrorism,' whether or not there is a basis for considering the targeted person a suspect or a foreign agent."[25]

Many critics of the Patriot Act believed the broad powers to conduct clandestine searches were dangerous and unnecessary. They said the government already had broad enough power to conduct secret searches in international terrorism cases under the Foreign Intelligence Surveillance Act. More troubling, they argued, was the fact that new powers for secret searches contained in the Patriot Act were not limited to terrorism cases but could be used in any criminal investigation. Moreover, because it is often difficult for the government to identify foreign agents, U.S. citizens and foreign nationals could be subject to broad surveillance and secret searches on nothing more than the government's suspicion.

Also troubling to civil libertarians is the Patriot Act's expansion of the government's ability to obtain documents and records that under prior law would have been considered private. The new law, for example, allows the government to obtain the financial records of bank customers merely by stating that the request is part of a counterterrorism effort. The law similarly allows the government to obtain telephone records and student records. Moreover, while the government had previous authority to obtain records from travel-related businesses such as airlines and car rental companies, the government under the Patriot Act now has authorization to examine the records of any business, ranging from credit card companies to bookstores. It remains to be seen, however, whether the new powers will help or hinder the government's counterterrorism efforts.

An All-Seeing System

Even as many Americans questioned the wisdom of providing the government with so many new tools that held the potential to seriously erode civil liberties, various government agencies were attempting to develop antiterrorism systems that by their nature held the potential to completely undermine the privacy of ordinary Americans. One of the most controversial efforts to uncover terrorist attacks before they occur was launched by the Defense Department's Advanced Research Projects Agency, which established what it called the Total Information Awareness project. The goal of the program was to develop a powerful information-gathering system that could help the government identify terrorists while they were still in the planning stages of their attacks.

The program's objective, as stated on the Total Information Awareness Office website, "is to revolutionize

Visitors to a computer trade fair learn about the latest advances in computer and information technology. The U.S. government hopes to use the latest technology to identify terrorists.

the ability of the United States to detect, classify and identify foreign terrorists—and decipher their plans—and thereby enable the U.S. to take timely action to successfully preempt and defeat terrorist acts."[26] The Total Information Office even had its own logo, which featured an eye atop a pyramid (similar to that found on the backs of one-dollar bills) overlooking a representation of the world. The logo included the Latin phrase, *Scientia est Potentia*, which means "knowledge is power."

Planners envisioned a system capable of mining a variety of databases, ranging from credit card records to airline ticket purchases, then analyzing the captured information for patterns of suspicious activity. In addition, program proponents hoped to connect domestic databases with those in other countries. In announcing the ambitious project in 2002, Defense Undersecretary Pete Aldridge said, "We are in a war on terrorism, we are trying to prevent terrorist acts against our country. We are trying to give our people who understand and try to track down the terrorists . . . a sufficient set of tools."[27]

Although many policy makers saw the proposed system's enormous potential to increase the government's ability to track and apprehend terrorists before they strike, critics complained that the program would seriously undermine civil liberties and privacy for American citizens. William Safire, a conservative columnist for the *New York Times*, noted that the program held the potential to track every American's every move. He wrote:

> Every purchase you make with a credit card, every magazine subscription you buy and medical prescription you fill, every Web site you visit and e-mail you send or receive, every academic grade you receive, every bank deposit you make, every trip you book and every event you attend—all these transactions and communications will go into what the Defense Department describes as "a virtual, centralized grand database".[28]

Because of the potential of such a system to snoop on ordinary Americans and to pry into intimate details of their lives, in 2002, Congress approved legislation prohibiting the use of the Total Information Awareness system against U.S. citizens. Nevertheless, many Americans saw in the Total Information Awareness project and in the Patriot Act the potential for serious abuses of civil rights and privacy. For them, the government's efforts to protect them from terrorism were a more significant threat than that posed by the terrorists themselves. While most citizens believed the government acted out of a genuine desire to thwart trouble, many were left to wonder whether antiterrorism efforts themselves would more effectively destroy terrorists or their cherished American ideals.

Chapter Five

A Changing Way of Life

In large part, the September 11 terrorists were successful in carrying out their plans because they were able to take advantage of the United States' open and diverse society. Blending in as students, customers, residents, and travelers, they were able to quietly plan their attack without drawing attention to themselves. After the attacks, Americans came to understand that their very way of life might be their biggest weakness. Indeed, the very openness of American society and the easy mobility of Americans—traits that have helped define the nation—may be among the casualties of the war. Restrictions on access to public buildings and even public spaces are among some of the many measures of the war on terrorism. While many of those steps do not represent an infringement on civil liberties, they do reflect a fundamental rethinking of America's open society and the tensions inherent between a country that is easy to access and one that is vulnerable to terrorist attacks.

More Searches and Reduced Access

In ways both large and small, the everyday lives of Americans were significantly altered by the nation's response to September 11. Among the first and most notable changes is the increasing number of searches and checkpoints in areas that once offered easy and unfettered access. For example, prior to September 11, 2001, entering an airport was an uncomplicated and easy process; today it is more cumbersome, particularly when the government issues warnings of a heightened risk of terrorist attack. During these times, airport security may extend to roadway entrances, where officials may conduct random searches of incoming vehicles. While usually limited to visual searches, more thorough searches of some vehicles may be taken if inspectors' suspicions are aroused. Moreover, because a terrorist might attempt to load a vehicle with explosives, then try to detonate it near busy terminal entrances, many airports have closed off access to parking near terminals.

Enhanced security measures, and a resulting decrease in freedom of mobility, also have changed the face of some of the nation's great public spaces and monuments. Many of America's most cherished and visited landmarks are no longer places where Americans can come and go freely. Airport-type security measures are now in effect at high-profile national monuments, at risk because they are inviting, symbolic targets for terrorists to strike. The Statue of Liberty in New York City; the Washington Monument and the White House in Washington, D.C.; the Gateway Arch in St. Louis, Missouri; and the Liberty Bell pavilion in Philadelphia, Pennsylvania, all instituted heightened security measures after the 2001 terrorist attacks.

Among other things, the National Park Service began the use of metal detectors, bag searches, and even bomb-sniffing dogs in order to ensure that terrorists did not attempt to attack these rich American symbols. All five sites were briefly closed to the public following the 2001 attacks and were reopened only after new safety measures were in place. The park service said the monuments, which are popular tourist attractions, would close down whenever the threat of terrorist attack appeared especially high. A spokesman for the park service explained, "The National Park Service is prepared to take appropriate action, as we have in the past, to protect public safety and preserve these monuments and memorials."[29]

Airport police conduct random searches of cars. National security tightened with the beginning of the war in Iraq.

When the government raised its assessment of terrorist threat to high in March 2003, security efforts were redoubled. In Washington, the White House was closed to public tours. Pennsylvania Avenue, which runs in front of the White House and had already been closed to vehicular traffic, was also closed to pedestrians. Only those with appropriate identification were allowed in the secure area around the president's mansion. Meanwhile, public tours of the U.S. Capitol were suspended, as were tours of Independence Hall in Philadelphia. At Mount Rushmore, in South Dakota, a number of parking lots were closed, and armed park rangers screened all vehicles entering the park.

Similarly, public access to prominent dams was curtailed. Whereas citizens could once drive across some dams or otherwise visit them to appreciate their enormity, the government placed restrictions on how close people could get to such structures out of fear that terrorists might attempt to sabotage them. For example, the road on top of the famous Hoover Dam in Nevada has been closed since the 2001 terrorist attacks and, in early 2003, the Interior Department's Bureau of Reclamation closed a public road that runs atop the Folsom Dam near Sacramento, California. The bureau, which manages 457 dams and 348 reservoirs across the nation, indicated that further restrictions might be necessary, especially at prominent dams such as the Grand Coulee Dam in Washington State.

Americans generally accepted the heightened security and resulting restrictions as a necessity in an age in which committed terrorists could destroy important American landmarks and memorials. However, as the terror and panic engendered by the September 11 attacks recedes in the national memory, it remains uncertain how many restrictions and inconveniences Americans will be willing to accept—and for how long.

The Military in Civilian Life

Perhaps one of the most unsettling security measures to emerge from the nation's war on terrorism is the increasing encroachment of the military into civilian realms. As just one disturbing example, the U.S. Air Force is now authorized to shoot down hijacked jets that appear to be on course to purposely crash into buildings or sensitive installations, such as nuclear power plants. For the military pilot, the action would have to be taken even though he or she knew that hundreds of innocent civilians on board the plane would die. For passengers, the knowledge that their aircraft could be shot down by their own military is equally disturbing. At present, the air force authorization is nothing more than a theoretical matter. However, the presence of the military in civilian affairs is far more tangible.

In February 2003, as the United States geared up for a war with Iraq and officials feared a greater threat of terrorist

A police officer stands guard at the Capitol Building. Most Americans have grown accustomed to the sight of heavily armed guards patrolling potential terrorist targets.

attacks on Washington, the military put up a protective barrier around the capital city. Antiaircraft missile launchers were deployed around the city, including on the National Mall. The sight of the armored artillery pieces in the park, in which many museums and memorials are located, was disconcerting to many Americans who had flocked to the area for years to take in culture, reflect, fly kites, or picnic. Fighter jets and Blackhawk helicopters supplemented the antiaircraft missile launchers in an effort to protect the capital from a possible air attack. In the meantime, residents of New York City watched fighter jets patrol the skies overhead. Even though their presence was intended to reassure residents, for many Americans, the flights reenforced the nation's vulnerability to attack.

Key landmarks and important bridges also bore highly visible military protection. For example, armed National Guardsmen patrolled the Golden Gate Bridge area in San Francisco, a park usually visited by hikers and tourists more interested in enjoying the fog-shrouded majesty of the bridge and the beauty of the San Francisco Bay than worrying about a potential terrorist attack. Yet, because the bridge holds such a place of veneration in the hearts of many Americans, the government realized it was a potentially rich terrorist target.

The Nation Braces for Attack

Even when citizens were not confronted with a military presence, they felt the effects of the enhanced security measures. Workers from all walks of life found themselves faced with new security measures, ranging from increased car searches to training in the use of safety equipment they never would have dreamed of having to use prior to September 11. Federal agencies and Congress established or enhanced traffic barricades to ensure suicide bombers were unable to crash into government buildings. Many government agencies distributed gas masks and evacuation hoods to employees to

Nuclear power plants, like Three Mile Island, are feared to be potential terrorist targets.

provide protection in the case of a chemical or biological attack. Members of the House of Representatives were armed with handheld pagers to notify them instantly in the case of an attack. A number of agencies even searched employees' cars as they arrived to park in government lots. Private-sector businesses that previously enjoyed a more casual atmosphere significantly increased security measures in an attempt to foil potential terrorist attacks. Following the 2001 assaults, the New York Stock Exchange (NYSE) prohibited lunch deliveries inside the building, for fear that a terrorist could deliver explosives hidden in a food order. The NYSE and many financial institutions in New York City also have increased the numbers of guards and checkpoints, hoping to prevent a suicide bomber from entering the premises. At the same time, however, these measures served to fundamentally alter the work environment, making many Americans feel as though they were prisoners of their own security systems.

Around the nation, police stepped up patrols of bridges, power plants, and rail yards. Flight restrictions were imposed over some cities and even Florida theme parks, and planes were banned from flying over crowded sports stadiums. Blimps and planes toting advertisement banners—once a common fixture over sports venues—were prohibited. Many cities across the nation increased police patrols around local government office buildings and courts. Some limited public access to government buildings to a reduced number of

Members of the National Guard patrol the area beneath the Golden Gate Bridge in San Francisco on the anniversary of the September 11, 2001, terrorist attacks.

entrances. Federal government office buildings began requiring anyone entering to provide proof of identity. Homeland Security secretary Tom Ridge asked the states to increase protection of the nation's food supply, extending down to feedlots and meatpacking plants.

The heightened law enforcement presence around the nation ironically led many Americans to feel uneasy. To them, the heightened security had turned a once-open country into something akin to a police state where everyone is a potential suspect. Others, however, welcomed the high-profile surveillance, reasoning that terrorists were less likely to strike with so many law enforcement officials present.

Water supplies need protection from possible contamination. Access to water plants and reservoirs became very restricted in the wake of the terrorist attacks.

Water Supplies Protected

Just as many Americans once took for granted their freedom to enter public buildings without passing through security

checkpoints, Americans prior to September 11 largely took clean drinking water for granted. To be certain, environmentalists warned about the dangers of pollution, but Americans certainly did not worry much about the possibility that terrorists could sabotage their water. All that changed in 2001, however. As stated in a press release that announced a congressional hearing on protecting the nation's water infrastructure, September 11 changed "our concept of what constitutes a credible threat to the security of our nation's critical infrastructure. . . . Threats that previously had been considered low risk are now being examined and incorporated into emergency plans and procedures."[30]

Reservoirs, which once served as places where people jogged and walked pets, have become more secure, with public access limited or prohibited. The primary concern for these places is that terrorists could poison water in the reservoirs, sickening thousands. A lesson of how damaging tainted water can be was learned in 1993, when the water system of Milwaukee, Wisconsin, became contaminated by cryptosporidium, a protozoan. More than four hundred thousand people got sick, and some one hundred people, out of the system's eight hundred thousand customers, died. Although terrorists would have to dump enormous quantities of poisons into the water in order to have a harmful effect, the threat of water contamination remains real and restrictions on public access to reservoirs has become commonplace.

Terrorists might also poison water by reversing the flow of water into homes and businesses. Using a simple vacuum cleaner or a bicycle pump, a terrorist could create a backflow to push poisons into water systems. Terrorists might also blow up pumping stations entirely, causing an instantaneous loss of water for an entire population. Tom Curtis of the American Water Works Association highlighted the extent to which such a terrorist attack could paralyze a city: "[Say] one city has six giant pumps, and they're all in one building. If you crashed an airplane into that building or blew it up, it would cause half a million people to lose their water supply almost instantly. Pumps of this size must be custom-built and can take as long as 18 months to replace."[31] Americans came to understand that, in an age of terror, it was imprudent to take anything for granted, especially something like clean water, which is so essential to good health.

The Terrorist Threat and the Free Flow of Information

Ironically, many Americans began to worry that the nation's war on terrorism could potentially harm rather than protect public health in the long term. That is because one apparent casualty of the war against terrorism is the release of public information that could be critical to citizens' health. At its core, the debate over the withholding of the information represents the difficulties the government faces in trying to balance the competing demands of full disclosure in a democratic society and protecting citizens from terrorism.

An issue in the dispute is whether or not to disclose information used by environmentalists to ensure the safety of citizens from industrial pollutants. The Clean Air Act, the Clean Water Act, the Safe Drinking Water Act, and the Community Right to Know Act have all required industrial polluters to monitor their emissions and make data available to the public. Some support withholding the information, saying it could be useful to terrorists intent upon releasing chemicals into the atmosphere. However, environmentalists say that citizens have a right to know what dangerous chemicals may be made at nearby factories. They worry that safeguarding the nation from terrorism might even be used as an excuse to let industries get away with polluting.

Another important source of information already has been curtailed. Under the Clean Air Act, industrial plants are required to provide risk-management plans to the EPA (Environmental Protection Agency). Among other things, these plans are required to include documentation of the number of fatalities a chemical release could cause. In this way, they help companies and local emergency workers pre-pare for a disaster. Inadvertently, however, they also provide potential terrorists with a clear idea of the best factories to strike to cause an environmental and public safety calamity. The EPA had routinely posted such information on the Internet and in libraries across the nation, but after the September 11 attacks, the EPA removed the information from

An armed security guard at a nuclear power plant is one of the thousands of people working for national security.

public view. Doing so demonstrated the difficulties the government faces in trying to balance the competing demands of full disclosure in a democratic society and protecting citizens from terrorism.

Fatalism Creeps In

As the nation's war on terrorism progressed, many Americans began to develop a sense of fatalism, believing that the worst was inevitable regardless of any precautions taken. Despite the intrusions on their privacy and their loss of mobility in the name of heightened security, Americans believed the chances that terrorists would find a way to strike another deadly blow against the United States were good. Even Tom Ridge, the secretary of the Homeland Security Department, warned that it was highly likely that terrorists would carry out suicide bombings in the United States, similar to those that have rocked places like Israel. In a television interview on March 13, 2003, Ridge said, "The No. 1 thing we seek to do is to prevent any kind of terrorist attack, but that lone wolf, that isolated suicide bomber might be the most difficult to protect against. We'll never be immune from those kinds of attacks."[32]

Such statements, coupled with some of the advice the department provided Americans, created an atmosphere of fear and panic among many citizens, especially after the government urged all Americans to assemble disaster supply kits. Among other things, the department said supplies should include three days worth of nonperishable food and water, including a gallon of water a day for each person, flashlights, battery-powered radios, first-aid kits, cash, identification, extra clothing, bedding, prescription medications, and pet food. In addition, the department urged Americans to gather items that could help families protect themselves from possible contamination. For example, the department said households should gather plastic sheeting and duct tape, which could be used to seal a room from contamination in the event of a chemical attack. Hundreds of people greeted

President Bush speaks about homeland security at Mount Rushmore in 2002. The Bush administration is working to maintain tight national security while preserving the American way of life.

the advice with panic, descending upon hardware stores to stock up on plastic sheeting and duct tape to prepare for attacks they hoped would never come.

The warning signified that American life had changed inalterably. The country's open society made it vulnerable to attacks in a variety of places, and Americans came to understand that they would never again enjoy a life as carefree as they had prior to the September 11 tragedy. Americans saw their society closing up in many fundamental ways, making them question whether terrorists had already achieved a victory of sorts by changing the way Americans lived.

The Costs of Security

The Bush administration quickly recognized that many of the security measures put into place since 2001 have significantly eroded the privacy and liberties of Americans, increased inconvenience, and cost the nation work time. The difficult task facing the government was to find a way to balance the need for security against a constantly changing foe while preserving the

American way of life. John Graham, director of regulatory affairs for the White House Office of Management and Budget, said it might be possible to analyze the trade-offs and come up with less intrusive means of preserving security. He said, "People are willing to accept some burdens, some intrusion on their privacy and some inconvenience. But I want to make sure that people can see these intangible burdens. . . . We can all see that life has changed since September 11. Simply identifying some of these costs will help understand them and get people to think about alternatives that might reduce those costs."[33]

Americans have long understood that wars require sacrifice. However, Americans quickly learned that the war against terror would be significantly different from any war in the nation's history. Moreover, they discovered that the weapons used to fight terrorism held the potential to significantly impact their lives, fundamentally altering society's openness. To date, the nation, by and large, has accepted the heightened security of the antiterrorism measures, which impose limits on their mobility and privacy. How long Americans will tolerate these and other restrictions, however, remains an open question. One thing is clear: Life in the United States has been fundamentally affected by the 2001 terrorist attacks, and the threat of future terrorism will no doubt continue to shape society in the years ahead.

Notes

Introduction: America Under Fire: A History of Response

1. William H. Rehnquist, *All the Laws but One: Civil Liberties in Wartime*. New York: Alfred A. Knopf, 1998, p. 218.

Chapter One: Safeguarding the Nation's Transportation System

2. Transportation Security Administration, "Baggage Security Checkpoints," n.d. http://129.33.119.130/public/display?theme=53.

3. Quoted in *Wired News*, "Due Process Vanishes in Think Air," Lycos Wired News, April 8, 2003. www.wired.com.

4. General Accounting Office, "Aviation Security: Registered Traveler Program Policy and Implementation Issues: GAO-03-253," November 2002. www.gao.gov.

5. Quoted in CBS News, "Bulletproof Cockpit Doors a Reality," April 4, 2003. www.cbsnews.com.

6. Quoted in CNN, "House votes to allow guns in cockpit; Trial period would require 250 deputized pilots," July 11, 2002. www.cnn.com.

7. Quoted in Scott Lindlaw, "Bush administration plans test program of guns in cockpit," *North County Times*, September 5, 2002. www.nctimes.net.

8. Charles Schumer, "Schumer: Inadequate Security Poses Severe Terrorist Threat to NY, US Ports," U.S. Senate Website, December 9, 2001. www.senate.gov.

Chapter Two: Bracing for Biological, Chemical, and Nuclear Terror

9. Quoted in Rob Schmitz, "Bush's Bioshield reignites research," Minnesota Public Radio, January 30, 2003. http://news.mpr.org.

Chapter Three: Racial Profiling and the Battle Against Terrorism

10. Quoted in Tom Infield, Diego Ibarguen, and Martin Merzer, "Defenses bolstered around U.S. capital," *Fort Worth Star-Telegram*, February 13, 2003, p. 1A.

11. Bureau of Citizenship and Immigration Services, "Remarks of Deputy Attorney General Larry Thompson," September 14, 2002. www.immigration.gov.

12. U.S. Department of Justice, "Final Rule for Student and Exchange Visitor Information System Announced," December 11, 2002. www.usdoj.gov.

13. U.S. Department of Justice, "Prepared Remarks of Attorney General John Ashcroft, Senate Judiciary Committee Hearing: 'The Terrorist Threat: Working Together to Protect America,'" March 4, 2003. www.usdoj.gov.

14. Quoted in Douglas Farah and John Mintz, "U.S. Trails Va. Muslim Money, Ties," *Washington Post*, October 7, 2002. www.washingtonpost.com.

15. Quoted in Farah and Mintz, "U.S. Trails Va. Muslim Money, Ties."

16. Quoted in Robert A. Levy, "Profiling Proposal: A rational and moral framework," National Review Online, October 5, 2001. www.nationalreview.com.

17. Quoted in Geoffrey A. Campbell, "A lesson to learn," *Fort Worth Star-Telegram*, October 8, 2001, p. 11B.

18. Quoted in Gail Russell Chaddock, "Debate over racial profiling intensifies on the Hill," *Christian Science Monitor*, October 4, 2001. www.csmonitor.com.

19. U.S. Department of Transportation, "Remarks for the Honorable Norman Y. Mineta, U.S. Secretary of Transportation, Arab Community Center, Cobo Hall Conference Center, Detroit, Michigan, April 20, 2002." www.dot.gov.

20. Quoted in Chaddock, "Debate over racial profiling intensifies on the Hill."

21. U.S. Department of Justice, Civil Rights Division, "Presidential Remarks." www.usdoj.gov. September 17, 2001.

22. Quoted in Niraj Warikoo, "Racial Profiling: Muslims and Arab Americans see their civil rights eroded," *Detroit Free Press*, October 24, 2001. www.freep.com.

Chapter Four: A Consolidation of Power

23. Stephen J. Schulhofer, *The Enemy Within: Intelligence Gathering, Law Enforcement, and Civil Liberties in the Wake of September 11*. New York: Century Foundation, 2002, p. 51.

24. Quoted in Schulhofer, *The Enemy Within*, p. 32.

25. Quoted in Schulhofer, *The Enemy Within*, p. 40.

26. Information Awareness Office, "TIA Overview (vision)." www.darpa.mil/iao/TIASystems.htm.

27. Quoted in CNN, "Military intelligence system draws controversy," November 20, 2002. http//cnn.usnews.printthis.clickability.com.

28. William Safire, "You Are a Suspect," the *New York Times*, November 14, 2002.

Chapter Five: A Changing Way of Life

29. Quoted in John Heilprin, "Protecting Parks from Terrorism," CBS News, March 7, 2003. www.cbsnews.com.

30. U.S. House Committee on Transportation and Infrastructure, "Terrorism's Threat to Nation's Water Infrastructure to Be Focus of Congressional Hearing," October 5, 2001. www.house.gov.

31. Quoted in David Isenberg, "CDI Terrorism Project: Securing U.S. Water Supplies," Center for Defense Information, July 19, 2002. www.cdi.org.

32. Quoted in Philip Shenon, "Security Chief Says Nation Must Expect Suicide Attacks," *New York Times*, March 14, 2003, p. A12.

33. Quoted in Edmund L. Andrews, "New Scale for Toting Up Lost Freedom vs. Security Would Measure in Dollars," *New York Times*, March 11, 2003, p. A11.

For Further Reading

Herbert M. Levine, *Chemical and Biological Weapons in Our Times*. New York: Franklin Watts, 2000. An overview of the history, development, and proliferation of unconventional weapons and their usefulness to terrorists.

Tom Ridgway, *Smallpox*. New York: Rosen, 2001. A detailed look at the history and devastation of smallpox.

Robert Sullivan, ed., *One Nation: America Remembers September 11, 2001*. Boston: Little, Brown and company, 2001. A rich pictorial history of the events of September 11, 2001.

Jill C. Wheeler, *America's Leaders*. Edina, MN: Abdo, 2002. Provides a look at national leaders, such as President George W. Bush, and the actions they took following the 2001 terrorist attacks.

———, *The Day That Changed America*. Edina, MN: Abdo, 2002. Provides an overview of the events and immediate aftermath of the September 11, 2001, terrorist atacks in the United States.

Works Consulted

Books

Peter L. Bergen, *Holy War: Inside the Secret World of Osama bin Laden.* New York: Free Press, 2001. Provides an intriguing analysis of the life and tactics of terrorist mastermind Osama bin Laden.

Editors of New York magazine, *September 11, 2001: A Record of Tragedy, Heroism, and Hope.* New York: Harry N. Abrams, 2001. A pictorial history of the terrorist attacks.

Thomas Friedman, *Longitudes and Attitudes: Exploring the World after September 11.* New York: Farrar, Straus and Giroux, 2002. Insightfully examines U.S. policy, foreign relations, terrorism, and the United States' response.

Fred Halliday, *Two Hours That Shook the World: September 11, 2001: Causes and Consequences.* London: Saqi Books, 2002. Analyzes factors leading to the terrorist attacks and the impact those attacks had on the world.

Katrina vanden Heuvel, ed., *A Just Response: The Nation on Terrorism, Democracy and September 11, 2001.* New York: Thunder's Mouth Press/Nation Books, 2002. Essays on the war against terrorism by staff members of the magazine the *Nation.*

William H. Rehnquist, *All the Laws but One: Civil Liberties in Wartime.* New York: Alfred A. Knopf, 1998. Provides an intriguing and thorough examination of how the government has curtailed the civil liberties of Americans during times of war.

Stephen J. Schulhofer, *The Enemy Within: Intelligence Gathering, Law Enforcement, and Civil Liberties in the Wake of September 11.* New York: Century Foundation, 2002. Provides a critical examination of the government's response to the terrorist attacks of 2001.

Gore Vidal, *Perpetual War for Perpetual Peace.* New York: Thunder's Mouth Press/Nation Books, 2002. Thoroughly examines factors contributing to terrorism and the government's response to it.

Internet Sources

Dave Boyer, "Despite profiling fears, FBI won't do it," *Washington Times*, June 7, 2002. www.washtimes.com.

Gail Russell Chaddock, "Debate over racial profiling intensifies on the Hill," *Christian Science Monitor*, October 4, 2001. www.csmonitor.com.

Douglas Farah and John Mintz, "U.S. Trails Va. Muslim Money, Ties," *Washington Post*, October 7, 2002. www.washingtonpost.com.

Robert A. Levy, "Profiling Proposal: A rational and moral framework," National Review Online, October 5, 2001. www.nationalreview.com.

Scott Lindlaw, "Bush administration plans test program of guns in cockpit," *North County Times*, September 5, 2002. www.nctimes.net.

Charles Schumer, "Schumer: Inadequate Security Poses Severe Terrorist Threat to NY, U.S. Ports," U.S. Senate Website, December 9, 2001. www.senate.gov.

Niraj Warikoo, "Racial Profiling: Muslims and Arab Americans see their civil rights eroded," *Detroit Free Press*, October 24, 2001. www.freep.com.

Wired News, "Due Process Vanishes in Think Air," Lycos Wired News, April 9, 2003. www.wired.com.

Periodicals

Edmund L. Andrews, "*New Scale for Toting Up Lost Freedom vs. Security Would Measure in Dollars*," *New York Times*, March 11, 2003.

Geoffrey A. Campbell, "A lesson to learn," *Fort Worth Star-Telegram*, October 8, 2001.

Tom Infield, Diego Ibarguen, and Martin Merzer, "Defenses bolstered around U.S. capital," *Fort Worth Star-Telegram*, February 13, 2003.

Philip Shenon, "Security Chief Says Nation Must Expect Suicide Attacks," *New York Times*, March 14, 2003.

Websites

The ANSER Instititute for Homeland Security, www.homeland security.org. This research organization website contains a wealth of intriguing information relating to the war on terrorism.

Bureau of Citizenship and Immigration Services, www.immigration.gov. An invaluable resource of information about immigration-related issues, including new government rules for foreign visitors to the United States.

CBS News, www.cbsnews.com. Articles on global news, including the war on terrorism, from the CBS News division.

Center for Defense Information, www.cdi.org. A wealth of intriguing and timely articles related to the nation's war on terrorism, provided by experts at the research organization.

The Center for Strategic and International Studies, www.csis.org. This research organization website provides timely antiterrorism articles and studies.

Centers for Disease Control, www.cdc.gov. A comprehensive source of information relating to potential biological and chemical terrorist weapons and the steps taken to reduce the risk to the American public.

CNN, www.cnn.com. Online articles from the twenty-four-hour cable news channel, including information about the nation's war on terrorism.

Council on Foreign Relations, www.terrorismanswers.org. A helpful and comprehensive online encyclopedia of terror, including steps the U.S. government has taken to combat it.

Federal Computer Week, www.fcw.com. A comprehensive source of information about government computer activities, including efforts to track foreigners in the United States.

General Accounting Office, www.gao.gov. Provides access to a wealth of studies by the congressional auditing arm, including examinations of aspects of the country's counterterrorism efforts.

Information Awareness Office, www.darpa.mil/iao. Provides an overview of the Defense Department's efforts to develop powerful antiterrorism tools.

Office of the President of the United States, www.whitehouse.gov. Official pronouncements from the president, including comments and actions relating to terrorism.

Total Information Awareness Resource Center, www.geocities.com. An intriguing source of information about the Defense Department's Total Information Awareness program.

Transportation Security Administration, http://129.33.119.130. A wealth of information on government efforts to improve airport security, along with helpful tips for air travelers.

U.S. Department of Homeland Security, www.dhs.gov. Provides a host of advice on protecting the nation against terrorism, along with updates on government efforts to shield citizens from terrorist attacks.

U.S. Department of Justice, www.usdoj.gov. Includes a wealth of information relating to the war on terrorism, ranging from criminal prosecutions to speeches to efforts to combat hate crimes against Muslim and Arab Americans.

U.S. Department of the Treasury, www.treasury.gov. A number of press releases and background information pieces that detail efforts to freeze the assets of suspected and known terrorists.

U.S. Department of Transportation, www.dot.gov. Provides articles and links dedicated to the nation's war on terror, including specific steps taken by the department to protect citizens and the transportation system.

Index

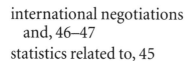

Picture Credits

Cover Photo: © Getty Images
© AFP, 30, 36, 39, 42, 87
© AFP/CORBIS, 57, 86
© AP/Wide World Photos, 16, 18, 20, 21, 38, 46, 54, 55, 58, 61, 74, 75, 91, 93
© CORBIS, 43
© Mark E. Gibson/CORBIS, 40
© Ed Kashi/CORBIS, 63
© Landov, 27, 50, 78, 88
© Lester Lefkowitz/CORBIS, 17
National Archives, 12
National Japanese American Historical Society, 11
© Reuters/Landov, 70
© Reuters NewMedia Inc./CORBIS, 24, 66, 67, 71, 82, 84

About the Author

Geoffrey A. Campbell is a freelance writer in Fort Worth, Texas. In addition to writing annual articles for the *World Book Yearbook*, Geoff also writes book reviews and op-ed pieces for the *Fort Worth Star-Telegram*. He was a research assistant for the book *Our Land Before We Die: The Proud Story of the Seminole Negro*, which won the Texas Book Award in 2003. He has written five previous books for Lucent, including works on the Pentagon Papers case, what it was like to be a soldier in the Persian Gulf War, Thailand, life in the United States during the Cold War, and the Lindbergh kidnapping case. Geoff is happily married to Linda, is the father of scholarly and athletic twins, Mackenzie and Kirby, and is a constant companion to two dogs and a cat. A youth sports coach and a frequent public school volunteer, Geoff relaxes by playing hardball in the Fort Worth Men's Senior Baseball League and in the Dallas-Fort Worth National Adult Baseball Association.